Mobilizing U.S. Industry
A Vanishing Option for National Security?

Published in cooperation with
the Institute of Economic Studies program

Published in cooperation with
the International Economic Studies Institute

Mobilizing U.S. Industry

A Vanishing Option for National Security?

John N. Ellison,
Jeffrey W. Frumkin,
and Timothy W. Stanley

Routledge
Taylor & Francis Group
NEW YORK AND LONDON

First published 1988 by Westview Press, Inc.

Published 2021 by Routledge
605 Third Avenue, New York, NY 10017
2 Park Square, Milton Park, Abingdon, Oxon OX14 4RN

Routledge is an imprint of the Taylor & Francis Group, an informa business

Copyright © 1988 by Taylor & Francis

Library of Congress Cataloging-in-Publication Data
Mobilizing U.S. industry.
   (Studies in American business and the international
economy)
   Bibliography: p.
   Includes index.
   1. Industrial mobilization--United States.
2. Munitions--United States. 3. United States--
Defenses. 4. United States--Military policy.
I. Ellison, John N. II. Frumkin, Jeffrey W.
III. Stanley, Timothy W. IV. Series.
UA18.U5U45 1988   355.2'6   87-34097
ISBN 0-8133-7573-8

ISBN 13: 978-0-3670-1215-1 (hbk)
ISBN 13: 978-0-3671-6202-3 (pbk)

DOI: 10.4324/9780429042010

Contents

Contents

Foreword

This book deals with an increasingly important, but recently somewhat neglected phase of our national security and that of our allies in the industrialized democracies—the maintenance of an adequate mobilization base and mobilization preparedness.

I view this topic from the perspective of one who has participated in the partial mobilization of American industry during the build-up in the Korean conflict and the early years of the NATO alliance and its full scale mobilization in World War II.

The combination of constraints in democratic societies, largely political in nature, on the size and scale of ready military forces and the new prospects for negotiated reduction and control of nuclear weapons with reduced reliance on nuclear deterrence places a new emphasis on the increasing importance of adequate conventional forces.

By the same token, these factors should focus new and increased attention on our mobilization base and the preparedness capability of the U.S. to augment its conventional military forces in being at the outbreak of any major conflict.

We must not forget or let others forget that we were once and could be again the "arsenal of democracy".

Totalitarian societies, ruled by dictatorships or small elites, are not constrained politically in building up and equipping conventional forces, as are democratic societies. Indeed, they can do so for aggressive or "blackmailing" purposes. Moreover, they can ignore or suffer the economic costs of this activity as well as the internal resistance to it.

Twice in this century the United States has had to embark on conflicts of global proportions, requiring full scale mobilization, because the imbalance of conventional military power in Europe and Asia threatened to result in a dominance in those crucial areas of forces that would be a threat to our freedom and democratic way of life.

Despite our demobilization in the wake of World War II we witnessed the renewed buildup and maintenance of armed forces of the U.S.S.R. far in excess of those needed for defense in a shattered Europe. These forces presented a clear and present danger to the democracies of Western Europe as the U.S.S.R. established and sustained totalitarian regimes in the nations of Eastern Europe.

For over forty years peace and security for the democracies of Western Europe has been maintained despite sizeable imbalances of conventional forces in favor of the

U.S.S.R. and the nations of the Warsaw Pact. This peace and security has been maintained by the nuclear deterrent and by a significant U.S. military presence on that continent.

The entry into an arms reduction and control agreement between the U.S. and the U.S.S.R. covering the intermediate range weapons of the U.S. and the U.S.S.R. on European soil seems likely, and an accord on limiting intercontinental weapons could follow.

This necessarily calls for a careful re-examination of the imbalances of the conventional forces readily available to the NATO command and the U.S.S.R. and the members of the Warsaw Pact. It will call for the taking of steps by negotiation or build up to cure any imbalances that are deemed serious by collective action of NATO members.

It also calls for a careful re-examination by the NATO countries, and, particularly, the U.S., of the state of their mobilization base and industrial preparedness and the adoption of a program to make them far more effective than they are today.

This achievement through continuing business-government cooperation will provide a necessary and desirable complement to our active armed forces and their back-up reserves. The awareness abroad of our industrial preparedness should strengthen immeasurably the deterrent value of our forces in being and increase the chances of maintaining the peace. Who can doubt the political and psychological value of a realization that the full strength of the U.S. industrial power can be readily and effectively mobilized, in the minds of our allies and friends? as well as our potential enemies?

In addition to the political difficulties of maintaining adequate active conventional forces and the need to compensate for declining effectiveness of nuclear deterrence, this book develops another reason for a re-examination, restoration and continuing maintenance of a mobilization base and industrial preparedness program. It points out the large amount of industrial restructuring going on in the "arsenal of democracy" and rightly observes that America's traditional industrial base has already rusted away, moved off-shore, or is being eroded by structural changes in the economy and strong foreign competition. Thus the mobilization-surge-rapid augmentation option is fast disappearing just as it becomes more and more vital to U.S. and allied security.

Besides supporting its analysis with illustrative case studies, this book suggests various approaches to "bridging the gaps", identifying the needed industrial and technological capacities, and makes recommendations for organizational reforms which call for careful examination at both executive and legislative levels.

These processes present no easy task. Time is an essential element. Three times in this century this nation has been severely challenged when our active forces in being were woefully inadequate and our mobilization preparedness consisted only of generalized planning with a bare minimum of existing operational machinery or legislative authority in place.

Three times we were spared the penalties of excessively long lead times that could have been avoided and, in other situations, could have had awful consequences. There, the oceans and the years in which our allies fought alone gave us the opportunity for meaningful mobilization of vast amounts of conventional military power and the creation of a strong mobilization base after our engagement in a major war was a reality.

In the third instance, the Korean conflict, a minor power was the initial enemy and our forces in being at the outset, with some limited help from allies, were able to sustain a holding operation until partial mobilization for any enlargement of that engagement to include major powers was in place.

The hostilities with North Vietnam in Southeast Asia were conducted with a gradual build-up of new forces and the redeployment of active forces in being on the basis of the application of the doctrine of limited force. It was determined that this approach did not entail a full or even a partial mobilization of U.S. industrial power.

No one engaged in the full mobilization program in World War II or the partial one at the time of the Korean conflict could fail to remember the long lead times involved in the mobilization process. Legislating the required authority, selecting and installing the expert manpower to exercise it, devising the necessary institutions and instrumentalities, acquiring the needed stockpiles, developing the detailed measures of government-industry cooperation and collaboration, and converting a large sector of the civilian economy to military production and supply while not damaging the channels of essential civilian supply—these mobilization activities took precious time.

Clearly it would be desirable to have much of the necessary framework in place to accelerate the actual production required to replace and expand inventories used in the early days of a major conflict and sustain the enlarged conventional forces needed to conclude the hostilities on satisfactory terms.

It is difficult to spell out for the layman, never involved in the scale and nature of the activities necessary for a partial or full mobilization, the time saving and other advantages of industrial preparedness.

Fortunately there are musty files that can give a picture of what it was like in World War II and the Korean conflict. In both instances programs were instituted for records preservation and analytical studies to provide a permanent record of these mobilizations for future guidance in similar crises.

The results in World War II are listed in the appendix to a volume published in 1947 entitled <u>Historical Reports of</u> <u>War Administration, War Production Board, Program and</u> <u>Administration Studies Series I.</u> A second volume, <u>Annual</u> <u>Series No. 2</u> was devoted to "Materials and Products" and a third addressed "Industrial Reconversion and Civilian Production". These volumes present the basic production record of the U.S. munitions program against the background of the production problems of business, the administrative measures of government, and the cooperation between the two. The handling of materials, equipment, utilities, critical common components and munitions production are treated in detail.

In addition, some thirty monographs in a Special Studies Series present analyses of the major policy and operating decisions in key industrial sectors.

As indicated earlier, the emergence of the so-called "cold war" with the need to establish a shield against Soviet threatened aggression and further expansion in Europe, leading to the creation of NATO in 1949, converging with the Korean War in June 1950, led the U.S. to undertake a partial industrial re-mobilization in the early 1950s.

This program was designed to increase the level of our military forces in being, to increase our industrial capabilities to provide for an expansion of our war-making capabilities, replenish our stockpiles of critical and strategic materials, while maintaining a viable essential civilian economy, and to join with our allies in enlarging our common unified defensive strength.

Many of the lessons and techniques of World War II industrial mobilization history were put to good use and some of the time lag and organizational confusion encountered in the early 1940s was avoided.

A striking difference and feature of this partial mobilization was its emphasis in its later stages on the importance of the readiness of armed forces in being and the permanent maintenance of industrial preparedness and an adequate industrial mobilization base for partial or full re-mobilization should either prove necessary.

This story is best told in short form in eight published Quarterly Reports to the President by the Director of Defense Mobilization beginning on April 1, 1951 and going through January 1, 1953. After the cease fire in Korean 1953, there seemed to be a steady lessening of emphasis on the importance of generalized industrial preparedness and the maintenance of the mobilization base. This was probably due to a greatly increased reliance on the nuclear deterrent in the middle to late 1950s and the 1960s and a feeling that any major war would be settled by nuclear weapons and, hence, be a short war.

The Office of Defense Mobilization continued for some years with limited scope and authority until a transition to agencies under other names largely concerned with civilian defense and general disaster relief. Currently, the Federal Emergency Management Agency (FEMA) is the repository of these responsibilities outside the Department of Defense.

In addition to the Quarterly Reports of the Director of Defense Mobilization to the President, referred to above, there are some fifty-seven specific reports, covering in detail the mobilization operations in some thirty-five industrial categories in the years of Korean hostilities.

Also, there are additional reports analyzing the conduct of more generalized program activities such as new facilities construction, tax amortization, emergency defense facilities, legal and legislative activities, small business, field service, production and distribution controls, labor participation, conservation of materials, mobilization base policy and program development, stockpiling, organization, consultation with industry and the like.

There are other more up to date resources for devising programs for industrial preparedness and the maintenance of an adequate mobilization base. FEMA's operations should be included as an initial point in any such survey.

Undoubtedly, the existing structure of relationships between the Department of Defense and prime contractors relied upon for procurement of needed military equipment for ongoing operations and adequate reserves provides an imporant base for undertaking programs of industrial preparedness, mobilization planning and the provision of an adequate mobilization base.

According to Mr. David Packard, the Chairman of the President's Blue Ribbon Commission on Defense Management:

"The DOD annually conducts business with some 60,000 prime contractors and hundreds of thousands of other suppliers and subcontractors". (See American Enterprise Institute Bulletin, Winter 1987, page 4.)

Moreover, the Industrial College of the Armed Forces has consistently maintained a fine program of study of various current aspects of industrial preparedness and mobilization planning.

The organization of this fund of knowledge and experience available from these various sources and coupling it with the necessary cooperation with private business to provide effective industrial preparedness is not a task to be deferred until major hostilities are underway.

Mobilization readiness should be constantly maintained as a basic element of national security addressed to these major areas among others:

(1) Preparing those companies and organizations already involved in military procurement for activating surge capacity on an emergency basis in the event of an outbreak of major hostilities.

(2) Making concrete plans for converting the millions of companies not actively engaged in military procurement to their appropriate role in the war effort while maintaining essential civilian supplies for the overall economy.

(3) Enlarging the productive capacity of critical materials and production equipment and the facilities supplying essential services such as transportation and energy.

(4) Providing the basic elements of civil defense.

In conclusion, may I repeat some comments in my last Quarterly Report as Director of Defense Mobilization to President Harry S. Truman on January 1, 1953, entitled "The Job Ahead for Defense Mobilization".

"Our ability to throw our great industrial strength into the scales of war quickly and efficiently is, on the one hand, a major deterrent to war and hence one of the greatest factors for peace. On the other hand, if it fails as a deterrent, it can assure us victory in the shortest time with the least loss of life.

Accordingly, we must make our complex industrial system ready in all important respects for the wartime needs. And since no one can say when that need might come, we must plan and take the necessary steps as soon as possible".

This book is a welcome addition to the increasing emphasis given in some quarters, official and private, to the importance of mobilization readiness for both its deterrent and military value should this nation ever be forced to wage a conventional war of major proportions.

It deserves the careful attention of those in this and subsequent Administrations and the Congress responsible for our national security.

Henry H. Fowler[1]

---

[1]Henry H. Fowler was Secretary of the U.S. Treasury, 1965-1968. Former Director of the Office of Defense Mobilization (ODM) and the Administrator of the Defense Production Administration (DPA) and the National Production Authority (NPA) during the Korean War in 1952 and early 1953 and Assistant General Counsel of the War Production Board (WPB) in World War II in 1941-44.

I Introduction

At the beginning of 1987 the White House issued a comprehensive statement of U.S. national security strategy that outlines U.S. security interests, discusses foreign policy and regional objectives, including defense and international economic affairs, and deals with strategic and conventional deterrence, arms control, and the need for "integrating a national security capability" now and for the future.[1]

Curiously, this comprehensive document received relatively little notice in the media, although it represents a landmark effort to integrate the Administration's views and in seeking to relate the various pieces one to another and to their larger whole.

Unfortunately, in its application of general principles the paper tends to gloss over major deficiencies in that very integration, such as the growing mismatch between our strategy and the resources available to carry it out. For example, the statement recognizes that the U.S. "must not adopt strategies that our country cannot afford, and that our military leaders cannot and must not base their plans on resources that are beyond the nation's capability to provide." Yet in practice, the government has failed to address systematically the linkage of resource availability to strategic options.

The force levels, programs and systems already approved or in the pipeline have been estimated to have a five-year cost of over $2 trillion (without any major acquisitions for the Strategic Defense Initiative or "Star Wars") as against only $1.5 trillion which the Administration projects as being requested from Congress for that period, leaving a shortfall of at least half a trillion dollars, even in the unlikely event that Congress provides all the funds requested.[2] This is simply too large a gap to be reconciled by the normal Pentagon processes of marginal adjustments, reprogramming, stretch-outs and even the needed improvements in procurement efficiency.

---

[1]"National Security Strategy of the United States," The White House, Washington, D.C., January 1987.

[2]See "Western and Eastern Constraints on Defense," cited below, and articles by George C. Wilson in the Washington Post, e.g., November 19, 1986. P. A 1

1

If not this Administration, then surely the next one is going to face painful choices in selecting a mix of strategic options which are compatible with available resources, which are constrained by political and economic factors. That such constraints will continue is suggested by the country's intractable fiscal deficits caused by government spending in 1986, for example, at a level of about 23.4 percent of gross national product, compared to the 18.5 percent in revenue, a deficit of 5 percent of GNP or over $200 billion.[3]

In an earlier paper published jointly by this Institute and the Atlantic Council of the United States, one of the coauthors addressed "Western and Eastern Economic Constraints on Defense: The Mutual Security Implications." It revealed the bad news that the Reagan Administration defense buildup simply cannot be sustained, absent some major rise in the perceived level of East-West tensions, and (in an appendix by Sovietologist John Hardt), the "good" news that the Soviet Union and its allies face analogous, though different, constraints on their own defense efforts. The conclusion is that if either side sees the other's problems as a vulnerability to be exploited, prospects of mutual and stable security will become more elusive, whereas if the common problems are perceived as an opportunity, in a positive sum context, significant progress on arms control and meaningful reductions might be jointly manageable with the new Kremlin leadership.

The present paper is a continuation of this analysis, and focuses on America's mobilization capacity—or rather its lack. The White House strategy paper notes that "the effective mobilization of manpower and industrial resources in the event of conflict provide an essential support for our military capabilities...we rely on the inherent size and strength of the U.S. economy as our ultimate line of defense".

In March 1987, the Deputy Secretary of Defense submitted a report to Congress on "War Emergency Situations and Mobilization Requirements," as required by the Defense Authorization Act, which noted the shift in the 1950s away from the traditional notion that "national security policy

---

[3]Office of Management and Budget, The United States Budget In Brief Fiscal Year 1987, Washington, 1986, Table 7 GNP was estimated at $4,206 billion, receipts at $777 billion and outlays at $980 billion.

and strategic planning have been based fundamentally on mobilization potential" to a recognition that "there may not be a long war to give our industrial potential time to bring its weight to bear," with a consequent reliance on forces in being. The Reagan Administration, by contrast, has emphasized the capability to fight a prolonged global conventional war and has thus given at least lip service to having "an emergency mobilization preparedness capability that... can respond decisively and effectively to any major national emergency...." This statement was followed in May by an internal memorandum from the Secretary of Defense stressing the interconnection between the competitiveness needs of Defense and the nation as a whole, which was reiterated by the Assistant Secretary of Defense (Production and Logistics) in July.[4]

Despite such statements of good intentions, however, government policy, on trade for example, appears to take little account of the profound transition in the U.S. economy over the past two decades in many sectors critical for defense. This decline in overall manufacturing competitiveness and capacity, and the possible loss of leadership in some high technology and R&D seems likely to worsen over time; yet the government as a whole is ill-equipped to analyze, let alone prescribe for this situation which includes but goes far beyond the Pentagon's responsibilities. Even the early Administration effort to provide interagency focus in an Emergency Mobilization Preparedness Board appears to have become moribund[5] under the post Iran-Contra reorganization of the National Security Council.

In consequence, there appears to be a lacuna in the cultures of both the national security planning community and the non-defense contractor business world in which each tend to ignore the other, thus avoiding rather than facing up to the many intersections between national security and economics. The business people, who believe strongly in an unfettered market system, and in fair, if not free trade,

---

[4]Statement of Dr. Robert B. Costello, before the Economic Stabilization Subcommittee, House Committee on Banking, Finance and Urban Affairs, July 8, 1987.

[5]A senior NSC official told one of the authors that "extant but on the back burner due to a lack of investment resources" would be a more precise description of the EMPB's current status as of September 1987.

often fail to factor non-economic considerations such as national security into the equation. Still worse, many business leaders seem to have adopted a short-term, quarter to quarter bottom-line mentality at the expense of longer-term strategic planning[6]. They often work to expand through the acquisitions game rather than by improving productivity, production and market share.

Both components of the military and industrial "complex" named by President Eisenhower have a strong cultural bias toward more sophisticated weaponry at ever higher costs. Their approach sacrifices usability and sustainability in the field and loses the intrinsic advantages of simplicity as the West endeavors to substitute quality for the superior quantity of forces and weaponry on the Warsaw Pact side. The United States initially put dozens of its most advanced naval vessels in the tense Persian Gulf region with inadequate protection against early-vintage mines!

In the career military, moreover, promotions tend to go with the higher-technology commands, rather than the traditional bread and butter forces and their supporting logistics or the less glamorous tasks such as mine sweeping. For the same reason, the military establishment tends to favor larger active duty forces and commands over reserve components.

In this short paper, the most the authors can hope for is to awaken the concern of the national security community, professionals in the Executive Branch, in Congress, in industry and in academia about the relevance of defense industry preparedness and mobilization capacity under the more likely scenarios endangering national security.

We hope to illustrate the dimensions of the problem, suggest the availability of cost-effective remedies, and outline some organizational and procedural reforms that might help the country to get a handle on this largely ignored but vital problem.

We will have succeeded if the subject gets on the agenda of internal Administration studies, such as the Pentagon Commission on Integrated Long-Term Strategy, if it contributes to the oversight functions of key Congressional committees, and if it is debated in the forthcoming

---

[6]This is driven in part by the "over-the-shoulder syndrome" involving fears of potential hostile takeovers, currently the subject of another Institute analysis.

political campaigns. We hope, too, that our efforts will help offer the 41st president of the United States some realistic options for dealing with the growing strategy-resources mismatch which awaits him.

This study cannot cover other important mobilization components such as reserve force structure and manpower or sea and airlift. We concentrate only on the industrial base aspects without devaluing in any way the significance of these and other related factors.

Our thanks go to Ronald Danielian and Nancy Thompson, President and Vice President respectively of IEPA, for their contributions and to Albert Toner, our patient and skillful editor. We appreciate also the assistance of knowledgeable organizations and individuals in and out of government, the support of Institute Trustees, and the financial help of contributors to the Institute, in particular the Federal Emergency Preparedness Agency. However, the recommendations in this study do not claim to represent official views or policies of that or any other government agency, or of IESI as an institution. It does reflect the joint views of the authors, who also take responsibility for any errors of commission or omission.

John N. Ellison   Jeffrey W. Frumkin   Timothy W. Stanley
Senior Consultant,   Senior Research   President,
IESI   Associate, IESI   IESI

II The Relevance of the U.S. Industrial Base and Mobilization Capacity

Government attitudes on this key question have varied widely over time. Following World War II, President Truman approved the policy paper known as NSC-68 which had as one objective "to provide and protect a mobilization base while the defensive forces required for victory are being built up". But under the Eisenhower Administration's "New Look", mobilization potential was subordinated to the idea of massive retaliation and initiation of nuclear response at the outset of a major conflict. The United States, of course, was then the dominant nuclear power.

President Kennedy reverted to the NSC-68 type emphasis upon conventional forces and, implicitly at least, recognized the importance of mobilization. President Johnson, however, elected not to mobilize for the Vietnam conflict which was attracting growing public opposition. This was unlike the Korean conflict, when controls and incentives were put into effect under the Defense Production Act and other authorities. The government thus had resort to some cannibalization of the Armed Services to provide men and materiel for Vietnam at the expense of readiness in Europe and elsewhere. It took the United States many years to recover from that drawdown.

The Nixon, Ford and Carter administrations supported the principle of mobilization but often ignored it in practice, and gave the higher priorities to non-defense spending, especially under President Carter.

The National Security Act of 1947, which established the National Security Council, the Central Intelligence Agency, and the Department of Defense (then called the National Military Establishment)[7] also provided for a National Security Resources Board at the White House level to bring resource considerations into strategy and force planning and to correct deficiencies in defense preparedness. That organization permutated under the Korean War stresses into a succession of agencies and the Office of Defense Mobilization (ODM) ultimately became the "czar" for production during the war, assisted by a network of satellite agencies. After the Korean War ended, however, these

---

[7]For a history of the origins of this basic "charter" see Timothy W. Stanley, American Defense and National Security, Public Affairs Press, Washington, 1955.

6

organizations were largely dismantled under various adminis-trations and evolved into an Office of Emergency Prepared-ness in the Executive Office of the President, whose direc-tor retained his statutory membership in the National Security Council. President Nixon, however, abolished that office and delegated its functions to the General Services Administration (GSA).

Later under President Carter the emergency preparedness and civil defense functions of the Department of Defense and GSA were consolidated under a new agency--the Federal Emergency Management Agency (FEMA). The loss of direct access to the President by the senior responsible mobili-zation official through the NSC appears to have been sym-bolic of neglect. This together with its lack of a superior policy and budgetary role in executive branch emergency preparedness activities have prevented FEMA from rallying support for its chartered responsibilities.

The Reagan Administration's national security direc-tives have sought both to restore the nuclear balance and to be prepared to fight a global conventional war of substan-tial duration. Indeed, one of its national security de-cision directives (NSDD-47) specified that the U.S. should have "an emergency mobilization preparedness capability..".[8]

Accordingly, an Emergency Mobilization Preparedness Board (EMPB) was established under NSC auspices to coordin-ate interdepartmental policy and actions and the Defense Department began to review the requirements for both partial and full mobilization, as well as to "surge" military and industrial capacity short of mobilization. But once again, principle and practice have appeared to diverge. The EMPB has atrophied and its functions fragmented to lower level working groups under the post Iran-Contra NSC reorganiza-tion; and despite certain planning improvements, mobiliza-tion requirements have remained at the bottom of the Pen-tagon's priority list, even during the years of the Reagan trillion dollar buildup.

---

[8]See the DOD March, 1987 report to Congress on that subject noted in the Introduction.

A comprehensive report to Congress by the General Accounting Office[9] looked at six weapons-system cases and found shortages of production machinery, testing equipment, raw materials, components, and skilled labor, plus reliance on foreign contractors and extensive waiting time for orders. A subsequent report on the erosion of defense-related manufacturing technology ("Mantech") found similar grounds for concern, given the small size and diverse nature of seed money programs by the military services.[10]

In summary, it would appear that the question posed about the policy relevance of mobilization is answered ambiguously, affirmative in the abstract, but unsupported by government funding and policy program priorities.

We believe that the case for "putting our money where our mouth is" rests on three basic factors:

(1) The probability that major conflict scenarios involving increased defense readiness and partial mobilization will become more likely over time, as contrasted with flare-ups or major attacks on vital interests with insufficient warning to respond with other than ready forces. An ability to respond to ambiguous warning signals without unnecessary provocation also adds a deterrent effect.

(2) An increased priority for non-nuclear or conventional capabilities in both U.S. and NATO force planning combined with the improving prospects for arms control that may be emerging. Any reduction of nuclear components, for example in an INF agreement, will place even greater demands on conventional defense and deterrence in Europe and elsewhere. It is also widely conceded that the most likely causes of conflict are a super-power clash in the Third World.

---

[9]"Assessing Production Capabilities in the Defense Industrial Base", GAO/PEMD-85-3, April 1985.

[10]National Academy of Sciences, Manufacturing Studies Board, Manufacturing Technology: Cornerstone of a Renewed Defense Industrial Base, Washington, D.C.: National Academy Press, 1987.

8

(3) In a political climate of "detente" and growing stringency in defense budgets, it would become increasingly difficult to meet the requirements to maintain and modernize the Reagan defense buildup and make high technology additions to the conventional component (such as the Follow-On Forces Attack strategy now accepted grudgingly within NATO). And the requirements exclude the enormous costs, up to $1 trillion, that could be associated with a deployed strategic defense ("Star Wars"), or even the less expensive tactical ballistic missile defenses.

Recalling the U.S. budget "gap" of at least a half a trillion dollars noted earlier, NATO's Central Region countries face comparable mismatches between requirements and politically available resources. In 1985, these six countries including the U.K., spent about $73 billion on defense. Even if this amount increased at 3 percent annually in real terms, according to a long-established NATO target, the $2 billion-plus increment per year would fall short of major conventional force improvement costs recommended by recent studies.[11]

Even if arms control does not prove to be a significant factor, the wide disparity between requirements and resources is going to require a major rethinking of U.S. and Allied strategies looking to the 21st century. While numerous alternatives could be devised, most of them would entail severe problems and risks.

The likeliest outcome in the authors' view is a quite different mix of smaller, high-quality active and mobile forces and readily mobilized augmentation elements and reserves.[12]

---

[11]See for example the report of the European Security Study, Strengthening Conventional Deterrence in Europe (St. Martin's Press, New York, 1983, volume 1) which recommended 7000 new missiles and rockets at a ten-year cost of up to $30 billion.

[12]See Leonard Sullivan, Jr. "The New Relevance of Industrial Preparedness", an unpublished paper, Washington, 1986.

If one factors in a possible arms control regime on conventional forces that neutralizes the Soviet blitzkrieg capability aimed at the heart of Europe, the West is revealed as driven to even greater dependency on mobilization. And since there is always a possibility that the Soviets might cheat or achieve a technological breakout, a combination of mobilization, preparedness and R&D would have to be kept in good order as insurance.[13]

---

[13]One of the most comprehensive rationales for mobilization is contained in Mobilization and the National Defense, H.L. Merritt and L.F. Carter, eds., National Defense University Press, Washington, 1985, especially Chapter II.

III Where the U.S. Stands Today:
Key Sectors and Case Studies

During the past two decades a profound transition in the U.S. economy has led to a significant decline in manufacturing competitiveness, and a growing weakness in domestic capacity. Numerous contributors to this transition include the globalization of economic activity, bringing sharp competition not only from such traditional industrial countries as Germany and Japan but from the newly industrializing countries of the Pacific Rim such as South Korea and Taiwan, whose economies are increasingly export-driven. The massive world debt crisis affecting developing countries in Asia, Africa and Latin American has likewise led to the adoption of import substitution and export promotion strategies, for example by Mexico and Brazil, with the encouragement of international lending agencies and the IMF.

Legacies from the oil crises of the 70's and high levels of inflation added to the world structural changes spurred by technological innovation, shifts in consumer preferences including a pronounced shift from manufacturing to services, and dramatic changes in market shares.[14]

American macroeconomic policy also deserves substantial blame. The twin deficits, fiscal and balance of payments, reflect the failure of supply-side economic theory to match government expenditures with revenues and the propensity of America to consume more than it produces currently about 104 percent of GNP, as imports make up the difference. Both deficits are sustained only by the willingness of foreigners to invest in or lend increasingly to the United States, making this country the world's largest debtor, with foreign obligations exceeding those of Argentina, Brazil and Mexico combined. Interest on our foreign borrowings is already

---

[14]For a detailed analysis and prescription for a more cooperative and effective world economic system, see Jack N. Behrman, The Rise of the Phoenix: The United States in a Restructured World Economy, Westview Press, Boulder, 1987, by the International Economic Policy Association. See also, R. Danielian, S. Rosenblatt and T. Stanley, U.S. Foreign Economic Strategy for the Eighties, Westview Press, Boulder, 1982, which found that the industrial countries as a group had "their real growth halved, their inflation doubled, and their productivity slashed" between the seven years before and after OPEC's 1973 escalation of oil prices. (Pp. 6-16)

1-1/2 percent of GNP and rising inexorably.[15] The growing foreign participation in U.S. debt and equity markets will inevitably lead to goals, objectives and managerial practices which may not accord with U.S. national security interests. This raises many questions relating to future U.S. mobilization capabilities.

Wide fluctuations in the dollar's exchange rate have exacerbated the problem for both the United States and its major trading partners. With the dollar overvalued, many American manufacturers lost market share at home and abroad to foreign competitors which is proving exceedingly hard to regain even though the dollar has fallen substantially against many currencies and reached closer to purchasing-power parity. But perhaps two-thirds of U.S. trade involves countries which peg their currencies to the dollar or, as in the case of Korea, refuse to allow them to depreciate in parallel to the Japanese yen. The U.S. is a long way from finding its way out of the forest of trade payments deficits. Domestically, Congress and the administration have only reluctantly come to grips with the Supreme Court's invalidation of the key GAO enforcement mechanism of the Gramm-Rudman-Hollings legislation which was itself a desperate remedy for the fiscal policy impasse between the Administration and Congress.

Finally, business itself has been characterized as fat and lethargic in meeting foreign competition, in improving innovation and productivity, and in adapting to structural change. Although the growing phenomenon of leveraged buyouts and hostile takeovers may have contributed to some trimming of corporate fat, management has been distracted from setting long-term constructive goals by the "over-the-shoulder syndrome" —the fear of a takeover which puts undue priority on quarterly bottom lines and stock values.[16] Furthermore, there is serious concern that much of the U.S. industrial leadership has lost its zeal for competitive entrepreneurship and is unwilling to expend the energy and

---

[15]This potentially dangerous situation is described in IEPA's The Forgotten Deficit: America's Addiction to Foreign Capital, by R. Danielian and S. Thomsen, Westview Press, Boulder, 1987.

[16]See R.L. Danielian, T.W. Stanley and S. Stuck, "The Impact of Hostile Takeovers on U.S. Competitiveness", International Economic Studies Institute, Washington, 1987.

take the risks inherent in out-competing emergent international competition. Whether this managerial malaise is a permanent feature of the U.S. business community is unclear at this juncture. One article describes the new CEO's as a "generation of ruthless management" eschewing "loyalty to workers, products, corporate structure, business, factories, communities, even the nation...With survival at stake only market leadership, strong profits and a high stock price can be allowed to matter"[17]. To the extent that it is valid, this indictment points to profound changes in the ethical underpinnings of American society that will affect our industrial competitiveness, our long term national security potential, and our "domestic tranquility".

Out of a host of potential candidates, we have selected industries according to two criteria: criticality to the defense industrial base, and significant declines in capacity, competitiveness, and prospects for the future.

This category includes machine tools, specialty metals, forgings and castings, bearings and industrial fasteners, electrical machinery and components, semiconductors, optics and instruments and certain strategic minerals. Petroleum and energy present yet another vulnerability, and doubtless, still other sectors could be added to the list, which is simply intended to be illustrative.

A researcher is struck by the inadequacy of available statistics, at least as collected and distributed by the government. None of the standard data bases and modeling capabilities maintained by Commerce, DOD, FEMA and other are comprehensively organized for the purpose of assessing sectorial capabilities to support surge, expansion and conversion requirements in an emergency. Furthermore, existing analytical resources are unable to capture the dynamics of domestic and international trends affecting industrial transition in the U.S. Therefore, this study draws on selected industrial base studies as a means of portraying these realities.

We have picked five industry sectors for case studies of the wider problem although, of course, specific problems vary by sector. Because minerals and materials are basic input to all industrial processes along with petroleum and energy, they are a good starting point. Although constituting only about 8 percent of U.S. GNP, non-fuel minerals are in effect, a sine qua non of the total national product.

---

[17] New York Times, January 25, 1987, Section 3.

But even if problems of materials availability could be solved, little would be accomplished if there is inadequate processing capacity; and here the case of super-alloys and ferroalloys are representative. Another critical stage in the evolution from raw material to end product involves capital goods, and a case study on machine tools is presented in some detail.

The machine tool case includes analytical methodology which might be applied to measure the capability of other strategically important industries to support mobilization requirements. Finally, semiconductors were selected to represent higher technology because of the availability of recent data from both government and industry sources and because this leading-edge technology represents a new class of challenges for mobilization planning. (A government report on the optics and instruments area is in preparation but has not yet been released.)

As explained in the introduction, the authors hope to increase the public and policy-making consciousness about a problem of national significance, rather than to detail all facets of the problem. We believe the following case studies will at least illustrate its dimensions and show the need for a more rigorous assessing of the national security-industry linkage in U.S. national security policy planning.

A. Raw Materials

The end of the Korean War marked the beginning of the end of a coherent national policy of industrial preparedness. Programs and agencies which had proved their worth in an actual emergency were dismantled and existing statutory authorities were generally ignored and rarely funded. Many observers believe that the National Defense Stockpile of strategic and critical materials, which goes back to pre World War II days, was frequently misused for political or economic purposes unrelated to its security rationale. It was widely alleged that the stockpile was used to favor certain geographic and business interests. Such allegations, even if not entirely valid, tended to undercut public understanding and support for the stockpile. Consequently, Congress set statutory criteria in the Strategic and Critical Materials Stock Piling Revision Act of 1979 and followed with the National Materials and Minerals Policy Research and Development Act of 1980.

Major studies of strategic materials have averaged about one a year since the Korean War. Almost without exception, they found grounds for concern over potential supply disruptions (in peacetime as well as crisis conditions) and outlined areas of action needed.[18] Little was done, however, despite the country's increasing dependence upon foreign sources of supply, including some of doubtful reliability.[19]

Paralleling this concern various bills have been introduced in each recent Congress, although only three of a comprehensive nature were enacted during the past twenty

---

[18]The prior studies included presidential commissions, executive branch and congressional as well as academic and business group examinations. The findings and recommendations of 33 such studies take six large volumes to summarize in a report done for the Carter Administration study of nonfuel minerals by Pennsylvania State University's Department of Mineral Economics and the International Economic Studies Institute. See "Issues, Policy Options and Recommendations Contained in Major Nonfuel Minerals Policy Studies, 1947-1977", Final Report to the Department of Interior (Contact No. J0188044), June 6, 1978.

[19]Chart 1, Appendix A shows the current extent of this dependence.

years. Similarly, Executive Branch studies have led to few concrete actions. The Ford Administration's National Commission on Supplies and Shortages did some useful analytical work, but assumed that the market could be relied upon to deal with most shortages, even during emergencies. The Carter Administration's extensive nonfuel minerals policy study led only to an abbreviated report on "Issues Identified", and follow-up was limited to a study of possible improvements in information and analytical capabilities.

The Reagan Administration established a Transition Task Force on Strategic Materials which submitted over 30 forceful but unpublicized recommendations. It was followed in April 1982 by a National Strategic Materials and Minerals Program Plan required by law to be submitted to Congress, becoming the first such comprehensive blueprint by any recent administration. Criticism regarding failure to implement the plan continued in Congress and elsewhere, however, and only the Commerce Department submitted in detail the various reports called for by the Minerals Policy Act of 1980. One response to such criticism was the Administration's establishment of the National Strategic Materials and Minerals Program Advisory Committee (NSMMPAC) in April 1984 to advise the Secretary of Interior with respect to both his peacetime and emergency defense mobilization responsibilities.

The International Economic Studies Institute has also contributed a number of studies, including a comprehensive book on Raw Materials and Foreign Policy.[20] This prior Institute work points out that the problem of making sensible and cost-effective national public policy in the area of materials has been complicated by the agendas of widely varied groups ranging from mining interests to environmentalists, many of whom have advocated extreme positions. Some people, for example, consider America's substantial and growing dependence on foreign sources threatening enough to warrant a national policy approaching autarchy, which would of course be unacceptably expensive.

Others, out of ideological preoccupation with the "free" market, or in opposition to any additional budgetary costs, or to any environmental damage, argue that the actual chances of supply disruptions, collusion by cartels, or other contingencies such as mobilization emergencies are so remote that no remedial actions are needed. Debates about

---

[20]Westview Press, Boulder, 1977.

U.S. policy toward South Africa illustrate the polarization of opinion. Those concerned mainly with a moral stance against apartheid tend to minimize the importance to the U.S. of that country's minerals, and vice versa.

The Institute's work suggests that there is a middle ground in which a limited number of materials do warrant policy concern, probably no more than two dozen, (compared with the 93 currently authorized for stockpiling and the literally hundreds used in different industrial processes).[21] In these cases foreign dependence might easily translate into vulnerability, so that cost-effective insurance policies are not only feasible but desirable. Cobalt, chromium, manganese and platinum are cases in point because of the heavy preponderance of U.S. imports from an unstable Southern Africa or from the U.S.S.R., the latter hardly a reliable crisis source. The U.S. depends on Brazil for two-thirds of its imports of columbium, and on Australia for about the same percentage of titanium. In that connection, the Soviet Union's blue water Navy and submarine capability, now with a global base network, pose a major threat to supply lines from overseas sources. Tantalum, Germanium and certain rare earth metals or other exotic materials should also be included because of their specialized electronic applications relevant to national defense.[22] In this latter

---

[21]Although glass is composed primarily of silicon, one of the earth's most common elements, Corning Glass Works found in inventorying its own supply vulnerabilities that some 450 different materials were actually used in the manufacturing of various specialty glasses. See T. Stanley "A National Risk Management Approach to American Raw Materials Vulnerabilities", Contemporary Issues No. 5, International Economic Studies Institute, Washington, 1982, p. 14.

[22]Some of these and related concerns were detailed for the iron and steel, copper, aluminum, titanium and superalloys industries in "Basic and Strategic Metals Industries: Threats and Opportunities", by the National Research Council's National Materials Advisory Board. (National Academy Press, Washington, 1985, NMAB-425). It stressed that a "healthy, technologically advanced basic materials industry is essential to national preparedness"; and it reviewed the many structural impediments facing these

(Footnote Continued)

17

connection the determination of new stockpile requirements should be open-ended to accommodate the rapid onset of new technology applications which often exploit new and exotic materials.

However strong the consensus within the materials community, an historic perspective on government actions tells a far different story. President Nixon, in effect, set a precedent when he changed the key planning assumption to a one-year war from a three-year emergency, which had been reduced from five years under President Kennedy, thus generating potential surpluses which could in theory be sold to reduce the budget deficit and relieve inflationary pressures. The present goals, based on the three-year emergency re-mandated by Congress, were established after a review by the Ford Administration and essentially accepted by the Carter Administration. As noted earlier, President Reagan submitted a comprehensive plan to Congress in April 1982 which reaffirmed reliance on the stockpile to meet military-industrial and essential civilian needs, in support of the national defense or in time of emergency.

Subsequently, however, there followed one of the most curious changes of course in the life of an Administration strongly committed to national defense, and rhetorically at least, to maintenance of an adequate strategic stockpile. Under the guise of a policy review and modernization, which most experts readily agree to have been needed, given the deterioration of some materials, the inadequate quality or form of others, and the need for more exotic materials for high tech weaponry, the Administration undertook an NSC Stockpile Goals Study. Established by then National Security Advisor William Clark's June 1983 directive, the study turns out to have been initiated by the Office of Management

<hr />

(Footnote Continued)
key industries. The Commerce Department's report (in response to the Ferroalloy Association's 232 petition) entitled "The Effect of Imports of Chromium, Manganese and Silicon Ferroalloys and Related Materials on National Security" (Washington, D.C., 1982) expounds upon the national security threat imposed by imports of high carbon ferrochromium and ferromanganese. Many of these same issues were addressed in the Congressional Research Service report on "The Competitiveness of American Metal Mining and Processing". (House Energy and Commerce Committee Print 99-FF, CPO, Washington, 1986).

and Budget (OMB) working through the Council on Economic Advisors and the Cabinet Council on Economic Affairs.

Until its completion in the spring of 1985, the exercise was conducted largely by mid-level civilians in apparent pursuit of a narrow and doctrinaire free market ideology and a predetermined goal of selling off stockpile surpluses to generate revenues for the budget. Although this study was interagency in form, the substance appears to have been largely set beforehand, under assumptions open to serious question by most objective analysts. Among such unclassified assumptions which the National Strategic Materials and Minerals Program Advisory Committee (NSMMPAC) questioned are: "that it would be feasible in a crisis to reactivate idle domestic production facilities... that substitution of alternative materials could be promptly undertaken... and that it is not necessary to include materials requirements for production of certain civilian goods which would significantly increase consumption of basic materials".[23]

Despite strong opposition within the Cabinet, which was somehow neutralized or bypassed by staff at the NSC-OMB-CEA, the White House announced on July 8, 1985 a proposed "modernization"[24] that would reduce existing stockpile goals from $16.6 billion, of which $10 billion were held in inventory, to less than $700 million, plus approximately $6 billion to be held in a second tier or "supplemental" reserve.[25]

Although the White House release of July 8, 1985 indicated an intention to sell off only $2.5 billion of surplus, the entire second tier appears vulnerable to

---

[23]Department of Interior "Status of Strategic Materials and Minerals Relating to U.S. Vital Interests", an assessment prepared by the NSMMPAC May 30, 1986.

[24]The writers are indebted to unpublished case studies of stockpile policy making by Richard C. Snyder a member of the NSMMPAC and by Dr. Ewan Anderson, a British professor at the University of Durham, made available to that Committee.

[25]Chart 2, Appendix A shows the relationship of stockpile goals to inventories over time, with all the implicit inconsistencies that have developed and the effect of the Reagan proposals, which have generated a considerable surplus for sales.

potential future sale, since it is described as "additional assurance", rather than a requirement as determined by the NSC study.[26] (In fact, it appears to represent a last minute compromise in deference to cabinet level opposition to the minuscule goals of $700 million.)

Inevitably, the Administration's proposals were greeted in Congress with skepticism and concern, leading to critical reviews by the cognizant subcommittees, the Congressional Research Service[27] and the General Accounting Office[28] all stressing that the proposals based on the NSC study were not an adequate basis for stockpile goal or other mobilization planning, nor by implication consistent with the intent of Congress in enacting the various stockpile legislation. Simply on its face, the absence of any platinum group metals from either tier of goals suggests the weakness of the Administration's approach. Yet despite its rejection by Congress, resulting in legislated restrictions on implementation OMB continues to press for the original proposal.

On the more positive side, and contrasting with the above, the Administration did purchase 5.2 billion pounds of cobalt from Zaire, the first such program in over two decades, plus bartering for over 3 million tons of bauxite from Jamaica, which was probably more of an economic assistance measure for a troubled political ally than a matter of requirement. Needed studies on stockpile quality are continuing, as is a program for upgrading ferro-alloy stocks by government swaps of materials, including chromite ores and manganese in exchange for ferrochrome and ferromaganese. A decision has also been made to purchase some of the

---

[26]According to FEMA's "Stockpile Report to the Congress, April-September 1985" Federal Emergency Management Agency, Washington, December 1985, p. 21 and Appendix V, inventory held which met existing goals was valued at $6.9 billion, with an additional $9.7 billion needed to meet them, of which surplus inventory could provide $3.1 billion

[27]"The Reagan Administration Proposes Dramatic Changes to National Defense Stockpile Goals", by A.R. Greenwood, CRS (86-578ENR) Washington, 1986.

[28]"National Defense Stockpile, National Security Council Study Inadequate to Set Stockpile Goals", U.S. General Accounting Office, Washington D.C., May 1987 (GAO/NSIAD-87-146).

specialized materials such as germanium, beryllium and rare earths for the stockpile.

Nevertheless, the impasse between the Executive, itself badly split, and the key Congressional committees most concerned, has in effect paralyzed most stockpile planning and program implementation for the past four years. Congress has acted to freeze all but a few transactions pending longer-term resolution of the underlying policy issues.

The defense stockpile is, in effect, a prepaid insurance policy against contingencies whose probability is hard to calculate, but which could impose severe shortages in the United States in the event of a mobilization-type crisis or even of foreign developments which had the effect of limiting access or escalating prices. Assuming that Congress will not allow the Administration to "cash in" this prepaid insurance, it is still clear that much remains to be done to provide a stockpile of key materials for modern military technologies in the proper forms and quality. Unfortunately, the unresolved debate about the content and size of the stockpile plus potential sales of surpluses has prevented critically needed action.

In February 1987, the Executive, as required by Congress, designated the head of the Federal Emergency Management Agency as the stockpile manager, although physical transactions continue to be handled by the GSA. It should also be noted that proceeds from the sale of stockpile materials are a potential source of funds for the general revenues but Congress has sought to restrict such use by the special Stockpile Transaction Fund and disagreements over the Fund continue between Congress and the Executive. It remains to be seen, however, whether FEMA's mandate can be effectively carried out in the climate of continuing opposition by the Office of Management and Budget and fragmentation of responsibilities within the Executive branch and the Congress. The latter did establish a National Critical Materials Council in the White House, which was implemented reluctantly and got off to a slow start--but may yet take on a new life with the designation of Interior Secretary Hodel as Chairman and the appointment of a new Executive Director who expects to work closely with National Security Advisor Carlucci.

The strategic stockpile is, of course, only one of the tools available to the Administration to deal with America's vulnerabilities. The Defense Production Act of 1950, which has rarely been utilized since the Korean War, authorizes financial incentives for additional mineral production, via price guarantees, purchase commitments, loans and rapid tax amortization. This authority, which also covers emergency

controls and priority allocations, has been periodically
renewed, usually on a yearly or two-year basis, as opposed
to the five-year recommendations of the Administration, and
it has rarely been funded. Even the obvious course of maintaining some stand-by capacity in both mining and processing, for example by small expenditure for water pumps,
essential maintenance and rail access, has fallen victim to
budgetary constraints.

The United States is richly endowed in natural resources, probably second only to the Soviet Union and
Southern Africa; and although the more accessible deposits
have been exploited, it is widely believed that considerable
potential for development in a case of national need exists
on public lands, where environmentalists have vigorously
fought efforts even to survey what is available.[29] Platinum
group metals, available only from Southern Africa and the
Soviet Union, can be mined at the Stillwater complex in
Montana and probably other places such as Alaska, but
production may well be inhibited by the overhang of a
potential "surplus" of 1.7 million troy ounces if the
Administration's deletion of this vital metals group from
both its proposed goals and the supplemental reserve is
allowed to stand.

Conservation and recycling offer potential for many
materials. Intensified research and development into
substitution possibilities has had at best limited and
scattered government support. Promising new technologies
involving ceramics and carbon matrix fibers, for example,
appear to warrant intensified attention. The recently
initiated program involving cooperative efforts by government, academia and industry to encourage new technologies in
superconductivity could serve as a model in the materials
field.

Actions could also be taken in the trade area, including selected subsidies and, as a last resort, protection, as
well as aid and other means of promoting diversification
away from locations where present supplies are over-
concentrated and where disruptions can be postulated. More
coordination with allies, including both key hemispheric

_____

[29]Currently this impasse is illustrated by the
controversy over possible oil development in the Arctic
National Wildlife Refuge (ANWR) in northern Alaska which
many geologists believe to have the potential of another
north slope.

producers such as Mexico and Canada and consumers such as Japan and major NATO partners, should also be part of U.S. risk management options—many of which may also apply to broader industrial preparedness issues, as outlined in later sections.[30]

However, if a balanced and cost-effective materials policy is to emerge from the welter of bureaucratic confusion, conflicting political and economic interests, and general public ignorance about the importance of raw materials to basic production processes, someone must exert leadership. That will require a decision that future contingencies are worth the time of today's decision-makers. One must conclude that the risks of substantial and growing U.S. dependence on foreign sources of strategic materials are manageable at reasonable insurance premiums _if_ the requisite efforts are made and coordinated central direction is applied. That theme applies to most of the defense-critical "endangered species" issues discussed in this report.

---

[30]The revitalization of existing but moribund resource cooperation agreements with Canada and the extension of such mechanisms to other hemispheric partners such as Mexico, Venezuela, Jamaica, etc. could contribute to a more assured mineral and materials security position.

B. Petroleum and Energy

Although Petroleum and its derivatives are very much a critical raw material—the base of the entire petrochemical industry, for example, the political economics of petroleum as the world's primary energy source are substantially different from the case of non-mineral fuels. This complex subject merits at least a brief discussion here.

The problem of looking at petroleum in a defense-emergency context is that the United States, while the world's largest consumer, is also the second largest producer, after the U.S.S.R. Assuming that emergency allocations were in effect, the defense need, which is relatively small in relation to that of the economy as a whole, could be satisfied without strain; and in addition to the Strategic Petroleum Reserve,[31] ample supplies are stored in the ground at various naval petroleum reserves. As stated in the DOE report, Energy Security, 1987, military demand for petroleum during peacetime has been estimated at 2 to 3 percent of the total U.S. domestic requirement. The combined militarycritical defense production demand during wartime has been estimated by IESI at 3 to 4 times this figure. Consequently, with the exception of uranium and measures to prevent bottlenecks in the production of special grades of fuels or lubricants, the Defense Department has played a relatively small role in national energy policy. This, it seems to us, is all wrong since virtually every defense production requirement requires a substantial energy input.

OPEC's successful cartelization of a critical share of the world's petroleum supply and price escalations in 1973 and 1979 indeed made oil a major national concern. Just as few analysts foresaw the rapid quadrupling and then tripling of pre 1973 benchmark prices, even fewer predicted the

---

[31]Despite currently low world prices, the fill-rate for the SPR is slower than many people recommend and it is only two thirds towards its ultimate goal of 750 million barrels which will not be met until after the year 2000 and could well be expanded to a billion barrels. However, the SPR which is administered by the Department of Energy (DOE) needs to be more closely integrated into DOD and FEMA emergency preparedness planning. Present plans call for the the allocation of the SPR by means of the free market price in a national emergency, which is of doubtful workability.

sudden collapse in prices in 1976, which caused U.S. exploration and drilling to fall off sharply with a concomitant shakeout of the entire oil service industry.

As the recent Department of Energy report to the President stresses, " lower U.S. oil production increases imports... raises the demand for OPEC oil, and Persian Gulf oil in particular... and increases the likelihood and potential severity of future disruptions in oil supply".[32] This, the report emphasizes, reduces flexibility in the conduct of U.S. foreign policy and "increases the cost of any new disruption to the U.S. economy". By 1990, depending upon future oil prices, net U.S. oil imports could approach 8 million barrels per day, nearly half of projected consumption, creating a higher vulnerability than existed at the time of the 1973 embargo! In fact, many commentators predict a return to OPEC price dominance in the 1990's with potentially serious risks to the entire world economy and particularly the industrial nations—the United States and its principal military allies. Yet such considerations are rarely taken into account by the environmental activists who fought the Alaska pipeline and oppose both ANWR exploration and shale development.

Even projecting as far ahead as 2000, petroleum is likely to produce 38 percent of U.S. primary energy consumption, measured in quads; coal and gas are projected to constitute about 25 and 20 percent respectively, with all other sources, including both renewable and nuclear materials, producing only 15 percent.[33] The extent of the vulnerability is clear; and, of course, the availability and price of energy for the U.S. are to a large extent a function of the world energy outlook and must take account of the likely acceleration in demand from both the newly industrializing countries and the developing world as a whole.

With the exception of regulatory (or deregulatory) actions and licensing or leasing, the government has generally preferred to rely on the workings of the market, so

---

[32]"Energy Security, A Report to the President of the United States", U.S. Department of Energy, Washington, D.C. 1987.

[33]Adapted from the U.S. Energy Association, "A Call For Action, an Assessment of the U.S. Energy Policy and Prospect", Washington, 1987.

that what was once a national energy plan, referred to in the dark days of gas pump lines as "the moral equivalent of war" now hardly exist anymore. A good start was made on expanding the strategic petroleum reserve (SPR), building a framework for cooperation with major OECD countries under the International Energy Agency, and beginning the development of synthetic fuels and renewable energy sources; but all of these supply side measures have languished, as have conservation and energy efficiency on the consumption side. Generally speaking, outside of the severely affected oil-producing regions, the country has rejoiced in the economic benefits of lower oil prices and the attendant reduction of other energy costs. This facade of abundance hides growing uncertainty as to the strategic availability of petroleum and effective allocation mechanisms.

According to the contingency analyses in this paper, such a stance must be termed short sighted, if not downright foolish, given the seriousness of the economic, political and military stakes. For example, the Synfuels Corporation, established with much fanfare and once lavishly funded, is in disarray, with project after project cancelled because any conceivable production costs are greater than the immediate foreseeable prices of the major alternatives, petroleum and gas. Coal production, once seen as a major asset, in view of the huge U.S. reserves, has also fallen on hard times.

Again, the analogy is a prudent insurance program where a reasonable premium is paid against possible catastrophe. The authors consider such a premium warranted. Alternative sources, especially synfuels derived from the enormous deposits of oil-bearing shale in the Rocky Mountains, should be brought to the best level of technical efficiency, regardless of cost, with the product purchased by the government for its own use, for emergency stocks, or otherwise subsidized. The same applies to all of the renewable energy resources, such as alcohol and biomass fuels from grain and from wastes. The U.S. and the Common Market produce large annual surpluses of both. The object is to have proven technologies and at least minimum standby capacity which can be rapidly expanded in an emergency.

Even more drastic measures may be worthy of consideration, given the volatility of world energy prices. The pros and cons of an oil import fee and a more general tax on consumed fuels have been widely debated, along with the notion of oil import quotas which might be auctioned off to the highest bidder. Here are major opportunities for reducing the intractable U.S. budget deficit by raising additional revenue, at the same time encouraging

26

conservation and arresting decline in the U.S. productive capacity. It is estimated that a 25 cent per gallon tax on all oil products, could keep gasoline prices below where they were at the height of OPEC's power and produce up to $40 billion annually. Studies by this Institute and the International Economic Policy Association suggest that a variable levy, similar to that used by the Common Market's Common Agricultural Policy to protect its domestic production, particularly in grains, would make sense if applied to U.S. oil imports, especially if rebates or other special treatment were provided for petroleum used as feed stocks, as contrasted with energy purposes, to prevent competitive disadvantages for key U.S. industries.[34]

The point of this discussion is to suggest that with respect to oil and energy the U.S. may be whistling past the graveyard of its economic and political-military futures. A defense mobilization or major surge contingency coinciding with a renewed world energy crisis could cause the severest kind of economic dislocation with major security implications. We conclude that oil and energy must have a high place on the agenda of a reinvigorated national system for mobilization and industrial preparedness.

---

[34]See: IEPA, "Petroleum and Foreign Economic Policy", Washington, 1975, p 23; "America's oil and Energy Goals: The International Economic Implications", Washington, 1977, pp. 23-26.

C. Ferroalloys

Ferroalloys represent a basic processing industry sector that provides essential raw materials to many streams of manufacturing. As a key component of steel manufacturing, ferroalloys are important to national security. By imparting unique characteristics to finished steel and cast iron and by inhibiting by-products which diminish steel quality, ferroalloys are irreplaceable to steel production. The principal ferroalloys of concern to defense planners are: manganese, chrome and silicon. Manganese is essential to the production of virtually all steels and plays a vital role in cast iron production, while silicon is used as a deoxydizer. Chrome as well as other earth metals are alloyed with steel to enhance durability as well as marketability. Ferroalloys and superalloys are good examples of basic materials essential for many critical defense and civil applications.

As of 1985 the domestic ferroalloy industry consisted of 17 plants employing 4,100 people with shipments of 700 short tons while working at 60 percent of capacity. In general terms this represents a 50 percent deterioration of the industry since 1978 when employment stood at 8,500 and shipments were in the order of 1,500 short tons. In the national security context, production capacity represents the most significant measurement. A 50 percent decline is evident here as well, with the 1978 figure of 2,136 short tons falling to 1,166 short tons in 1985.[35] Clearly, ferroalloy demand closely correlates with the demand for steel products.[36] As its largest consumer, a vigorous steel industry is in turn critical to the viability of the ferroalloy industry. The average ton of raw steel uses about 29 pounds of ferroalloys with carbon and alloy steel requiring about 14 and 34 pounds respectively while stainless uses approximately 450 pounds of ferroalloy per short ton. The 29 pound average is a reflection of relative contents for steel products.[37]

---

[35] The Ferroalloys Association, Washington, D.C.

[36] See Charts 3 and 4, Appendix A.

[37] The Logistics Management Board, The Effects of a Loss of Domestic Ferroalloy Capacity, Bethesda, Md., June 1986, p. 1.

As demand for domestic steel continues to be undermined by import penetration and a general malaise settles on the steel market, ferroalloy producers will continue to find themselves pressed to maintain production levels and will be forced to cut back further. The many pressures endured by the industry range from domestic macroeconomic imbalances to surging global production capabilities.

Ferroalloys as a Variable in the Mobilization Equation

Under any realistic emergency-mobilization scenario, the demand for steel and steel products will grow precipitously. Regardless of major innovations in composites and nonferrous substitutes, steel will remain a vital element in the production of war materiel.[38] It is estimated that defense and essential civilian requirements during wartime would grow 30 percent above current domestic capacity.[39] A strong demand for steel creates a concomitant demand for ferroalloy products. Using the 29 pound per steel short ton estimate and assuming that the 600,000 short ton ferroalloy reserve capacity is viable, the U.S. would still face a domestic shortfall of 14 percent of critical demand in wartime.[40] Presumably this shortfall would be met by increased imports provided that such imports would be available under the prevailing logistical and political constraints—including the challenge of maintaining safe passage through sea lanes.

Exacerbating the security threat of a production shortfall is the extent of U.S. dependence upon foreign ore deposits. Clearly the degradation of the industry and the inability to mine as well as produce from the same source

---

[38] Despite the obvious interdependence between the steel and ferroalloys industries, the former have opposed the latter's petitions for import relief, favoring the shorter term interest in cheaper offshore supplies over the long term interest in reliable domestic capacity.

[39] See Chart 5, Appendix A.

[40] Assuming a wartime demand of 141 million short tons, demand for ferroalloys would be 2 million short tons. Current capacity (1985) is 1.17 million short tons plus the 600 thousand short ton standby capacity leaving a deficit of approximately 200 thousand short tons.

are closely related. The U.S. has no chromium or manganese ore reserves. On a worldwide basis, about 80 percent of chromium and 50 percent of manganese reserves are in Southern Africa. This dependency may have an impact on national security during a time of crisis when sea routes may be blocked or shipping is unavailable. Additionally, domestic crises or foreign embargoes could undermine even peacetime supply reliability. The trend toward processing closer to the mining source is substantiated by that fact foreign producers supply over 90 percent of the markets for high-carbon ferrochromium and more than 50 percent of the ferromanganese markets while the U.S. ferrosilicon industry is supplied predominately from the relatively abundant domestic resources.[41]

Other factors such as subsidies, power, environmental standards, predatory pricing and inexpensive labor have equally deleterious consequences for domestic competitiveness. During the late 1970's and early 1980's foreign producers were able to make great inroads into the U.S. market while the exchange value of the dollar was disproportionately inflated and they have shown great reluctance to yield those hard-fought gains in market share. They have instead accepted lower profitability and lower returns on capital.

Competitive Pressures being faced by Domestic Producers

Although a global overcapacity for ferroalloy products is putting enormous pressure on prices, capacity is expected to continue to grow 3 percent by 1990 from 1985 levels. This trend is the result of strong competition amongst world producers to maintain market shares, which has flooded the U.S. market with low-priced imports. Another factor driving output is Third World debt, which places strong pressure on those debtor countries, the predominant ferroalloy producers, to generate hard currency and maintain employment. Thus the ferroalloy industry has been prominent in the industrial development efforts of such countries as Brazil, South Africa, as well as France.

This combination of forces places the prime incentive on generating foreign capital, even if the production source is economically unjustifiable under rational cost-benefit

---

[41]The U.S. Bureau of Mines, *Mineral Facts and Problems*, Washington, D.C., 1985 Edition, p. 265.

analyses. The major international lending and aid organizations have cooperated by providing inexpensive capital for Third World ferroalloy manufacturing development. Most of this production is for export, with a large percentage targeted for the United States. By lowering the cost of capital these favorable lending practices by the World Bank and IMF give third world countries an unfair competitive advantage over U.S. producers who must rely upon profit-making lending institutions for their capital improvements.

The greatest cost discrepancy between developed and developing countries in the production of ferroalloys is in the cost of energy. In the energy-intensive ferroalloys industry, silicon alloys require 10,000 to 12,000 kilowatt-hours of electric energy per ton of silicon content while the other major ferroalloys require 2,100 to 6,000 kilowatt-hours per ton of content.[42] Developing countries often provide subsidies to their domestic producers and in many cases they are able to provide less expensive energy owing to favorable access to low-cost fossil fuel, hydropower and other energy sources. Environmental regulations, often non-existent elsewhere, present a formidable cost for U.S. domestic ferroalloy producers operating in a very competitive marketplace. Environmental compliance makes up a large part of their capital expenditures and approximately 8 percent of the energy consumed by the industry goes to pollution-control devices.[43]

Imports

Imports from 1979 to 1985 have increased from 45% of apparent consumption to over 60 percent. Since 1985 there has been no commercial domestic production of high-carbon ferrochromium in the U.S. and only very limited commercial production of high carbon ferromanganese is currently available. By contrast, South Africa, while being the third largest producer of ferroalloys, is the largest exporter in the world. South Africa has the greatest penetration of the U.S. market with a 28 percent share of apparent consumption

---

[42]Bureau of Mines, Mineral Facts and Problems, p. 272.

[43]Ferroalloy Industry Association, Washington, D.C.

31

(1984). France follows with a 8.6 percent[44] share and the trend is towards increasing foreign domination.[45] Dependence is greatest for manganese and chromium products while the silicon market is dominated by domestic producers who hold 70 percent of the market for silicon metal and lowgrade silicon products. Blast furnace manganese has not been produced in this country since 1977 owing to the easy availability of imports. This represents an annual capacity loss of about 1 million short tons.[46]

Another aspect of foreign dependence is the degree to which the domestic capacity is being dominated by foreign-owned multinational corporations. Over half of the U.S. domestically-produced ferroalloys come from non-domestically-owned facilities. Theoretically, during an emergency this capacity could be allocated or even expropriated to serve government needs, although DOD has shown some ambivalence about this contingency at least at the high-tech level as demonstrated by the recent Fujitsu-Fairchild incident discussed below.

Recognizing the implications of a foreign supply-dominated U.S. market to domestic capacity, the Ferroalloy Association in 1981 filed a petition on behalf of the industry for import relief under provision 232 of the U.S. Trade Expansion Act of 1962.[47] The Commerce Department found that a national security threat was posed by the degree to which the U.S. was dependent upon foreign sources of high carbon ferrochromium and high carbon ferromanganese. Presented with this finding the President is given wide discretion on how to respond as long as the response mitigates the threat. The Administration decided on a program aimed at supporting the domestic industry which includes:[48]

---

[44]While French imports account for over 20 percent of the ferromanganese market, France does not have an indigenous ore supply.

[45]Ferroalloy Industry Association.

[46]Bureau of Mines.

[47]See section on machine tools.

[48]United States Department of Commerce, U.S. Industrial Outlook 1986, Washington, D.C., p. 19-5.

1) Conversion of Government-owned manganese and chromium ore reserves to ferroalloys by domestic firms for the strategic stockpile; and

2) Removing high-carbon ferromanganese products exported by less developed countries from the U.S. list of products eligible for Generalized System of Preference (GSP) tariff treatment.

Subsequently, DOD sponsored an initiative which placed stipulations on defense contractors requiring them with certain exceptions to purchase products fabricated from domestic ferrochromium.

In addition to the loss of production capacity and increasing foreign control there are growing indications that U.S. industrial firms that support the ferroalloy sector are contracting or disappearing altogether. The suppliers of heavy machinery, replacement parts and field engineering services and refractory materials have substantially given way to foreign competition in recent years. The shrinkage in these support subsectors parallels the attrition in basic ferroalloy capacity in the U.S. and follows a pattern of foreign-based sourcing as ownership shifts to foreign control. In any case the basic industry diminution as well as the supplier shrinkage places national security interests at risk.

Outlook

The immediate trend is toward further shifting of ferroalloy production capacity from nations that consume most of the output to developing countries where the raw materials are found. The reasons for this as detailed above are:

1) Weak demand, which is primarily the result of a shrinking domestic steel industry.

2) The difficulty domestic producers have in competing against imports owing to relatively higher input costs (i.e. energy and labor).

3) Environmental standards that place a burden on domestic producers not found at the third world level. Pollution control absorbs much of the capital investment resources needed for modernization and R&D.

Imports have supplanted domestic capacity of ferro-maganese and ferrochromium products to such an extent that the industry has become almost solely dependent upon silicon for its survival. However, imports of silicon products have increased significantly since 1980 although they have leveled off in the past few years. If they should regain their momentum the survival of the entire domestic ferro-alloy industry could be in jeopardy.

The unique structure of the industry has contributed to its competitiveness problems: the industry is dominated by relatively small producers and diversification and vertical integration are minimal. These factors have increased risk, inhibited investment and constrained needed R&D because of a lack of transferable financial resources, making the indus-try extremely unstable during periods of market recession.[49]

As indicated above, energy costs play a vital role in determining the competitive disposition of domestic silicon producers. In the U.S., energy costs account for 30 to 40 percent of the total cost of ferrosilicon and silicon metal. The outlook is that relative to the rest of the world the U.S. will be in the mid-range of energy costs according to currently quoted rates from major ferroalloy-producing regions of the country.[50] Our energy position vis a vis the Third World should remain stable, and foreign source depen-dency there is not a problem as domestic ferroalloys pro-ducers have ample access to indigenous coal resources. Countries with ore resources as well as production capacity will be in the strongest position as the trend is for continued vertical integration and growing sophistication of output. Countries now mining and processing for slab will shift to exporting higher value-added products such as stainless steel.

This trend will favor production expansion in many of the countries already responsible for much of the world's current output, including South Africa and Brazil, as well as many nations with tremendous potential which has been unmet for non-economic reasons (i.e. political instability) such as India and the Philippines. Thus, states which have

---

[49]National Research Council, National Materials Advisory Board, Basic and Strategic Metals Industries: Threats and Opportunities, National Academy Press, Washington, D.C., 1985.

[50]Bureau of Mines, Mineral Facts and Problems, p. 274.

an inexpensive indigenous source of fuel as well as a ferroalloy ore and processing capacity with few ecological restrictions will have the greatest advantage. But those dependent upon imported fuel or imported ore—most of the traditional steel-producers including the United States, Japan and Western Europe—will face growing pressure to reduce ferroalloy-producing capacity.

Furthermore, the government program of converting ore to ferroalloys for the strategic stockpile while providing a limited source of revenue for a much beleaguered industry, does not significantly mitigate the threat to national security. In reality, the stockpile conversion program may do little to make the industry more competitive in a global context and could precipitate a cycle of growing dependency between ferroalloy producers and the federal government.

The benefits of the program are:[51]

1) A temporary stimulus to domestic producers of ferroalloys which will provide economic returns while maintaining capacity during a period of slack demand.

2) Upon completion the nation will have an independent supply and stockpile of two major ferroalloys should a national emergency be declared regardless of the state of the industry at that time.

Disadvantages include:

1) The budgetary cost of the conversion, originally planned to be funded by stockpile sales of excess commodities; but since such disposals, e.g. tin, silver, etc., are controversial, the relatively modest costs are to be paid from the Stockpile Transition Fund.

2) The utility of the stockpile additions may deteriorate as technological changes affect the way in which steel is produced.

3) By providing a guaranteed source of income, at least temporarily, to maintain capacity, the government is providing little incentive for the industry to modernize or invest in R&D which is essential for improved long term

---

[51]Bureau of Mines, Mineral Facts and Problems, p. 272.

productivity if the industry is to succeed in global competition. The fact that the stockpile conversion is of finite duration minimizes the incentive to invest in capital improvements.

At the end of the program the industry might actually find itself worse off because it will not be competitive by virtue of its government dependency. The federal government faced with the prospect of an industry which would be almost helpless in the global arena would be forced to create a system of permanent subsidies or rely on the options of expropriation or government operation or total reliance on foreign sources for the mobilization contingency.

Some experts believe that if current trends continue, by 1991 there will be no domestically owned ferroalloy production facility in the United States! Consequently, growing interest is being expressed in submitting another Section 232 national security petition in recognition of the rapid deterioration of the industry since 1981.[52] Regardless of the industry's actions, mobilization planners are going to have to consider the implications of a foreign-owned domestic ferroalloy production capacity which falls short of wartime requirements for U.S. national security. Certainly, the present situation presents a threat as substantiated by the Commerce Departments findings. The Administration's program should help to alleviate the short-term consequences of that threat but will do little to remedy structural deficiencies.

In contrast to the U.S. situation, the imperative of having a stable ferroalloy capability is recognized by the major industrially developed countries. The Japanese and EEC have taken measures to protect their ferroalloy capacity from imports.[53] The EEC has established a minimum price standard for all ferroalloy imports in order to protect

---

[52] See Chart 6, Appendix A.

[53] In May of 1983 at the "Infacon" meeting in Japan, Mr. Eishiro Saito, Chairman of the Japan Iron and Steel Foundation and of Nippon Steel stated "I would like to emphasize that in view of the importance of the ferroalloy industry to the national economy as a whole and the need to maintain and develop national security and technology, every nation must keep its ferroalloy industry viable, at an appropriate scale", The Ferroalloy Association, Washington, D.C.

European capacity. Given the steady deterioration of the
industry since the first 232 petition was filed as well as
what present trends portend, the long-term implications of
growing foreign source dependence for U.S. industrial
preparedness remain to be resolved.

Indeed the ferroalloys case raises the broader question
of whether the system of "petitions" by interested parties;
which are then "litigated" under a quasi-judicial administrative law process is adequate. Rather, it can be argued,
the government itself should recognize and act upon the
national security implications of declining vital industries, assuming a proactive role rather than one of arbitra-
tion. In this view, the executive branch should initiate
systematic reviews of the "endangered species", make the
appropriate determinations, and seek to develop cost-
effective policy actions and managerial remedies. But this
will require sensitizing the policy-making community to
industrial realities and to the importance of a mobilization
potential, as described in other sections of this paper.

D. Machine Tools

The machine tool industry is an intermediate producer that provides essential capital equipment for a wide spectrum of manufacturing activity. Thus, machine tools are a critical component of any manufacturing process which must bend and shape metal or process metal from ingot to finished product. All fabricated metal items are essentially produced by machine tools. The fact that common components such as bearings and precision castings are produced with machine tools also links them to virtually all domestic manufacturing. The past decade has witnessed a significant deterioration of the domestic machine tool production capacity as imports displace many domestic producers. The loss of much of this domestic capacity presents the U.S. with a basic challenge to American manufacturing competitiveness and a significant threat to national security.

Consequently, the National Machine Tool Builders Association (NMTBA) petitioned the Department of Commerce in 1983 for import relief under Section 232 of the Trade Expansion Act of 1962. In an attempt to ameliorate the competitive disposition of the machine tool industry, Section 232 provides that any agency or private concern may request an investigation to determine the effect of imports on national security. Specifically, a two-step process is used to determine whether any action should be taken to adjust imports. First, the Department of Commerce determines whether sufficient supplies are assured given the defense mobilization capacity and the availability of reliable imports in wartime-emergency planning scenarios. Should the investigation turn up a supply shortfall, or if the need for a U.S. technological advantage calls for further investigation, Commerce then analyses whether imports have played a significant role. The Secretary of Commerce then reports his findings and recommendations to the President who in turn determines what, if any, actions are necessary to remove the import threat to national security.[54] As noted in the end of the ferroalloys section, the question arises whether such a case-by-case adjudicatory, rather than an initiating role, for the government is appropriate for today's conditions.

---

[54] U.S. Department of Commerce, The Effect of Imports on the National Security, Washington, D.C., 1984.

The contraction of the machine tool industry has profound consequences for the U.S. mobilization-surge capability. While the industry produced less than 1 percent of gross national product, machine tools represent the fundamental building blocks for war materiel production. As such, they are needed to manufacture almost all of our most critical war-fighting components (e.g. tanks, ships, planes, and transport equipment.) Even in a non-surge economy, almost 25 percent of the nation's total consumption of machine tools is linked directly or indirectly to defense requirements. In wartime, experience suggested that total demands on the industry will rise to levels six to eight times higher than peacetime demand, largely as a result of military needs.

The structure of the machine tool industry is unique in that it consists of hundreds of small to medium-sized producers with the top ten firms accounting for 75 percent of the market. The high degree of concentration is illustrated by the fact that while the average size of a machine tool producer as measured in sales is $20 million dollars, the median is only $10 million. Many of the firms within the industry are privately held and consequently do not file annual reports, while those that are publicly owned often have non machine tool-related subsidiaries. This makes compiling precise data on the industry difficult owing to consolidation in reporting. However, there is much evidence that the structure of the industry is changing rapidly with foreign-owned firms beginning to supplant U.S.-owned production in the domestic market.

In addition, some U.S. producers are directly importing foreign products while others are establishing offshorebased facilities. The majority, though, have sought to use joint ventures with foreign firms and manufacturing licensing arrangements in order to share the cost advantages of overseas production.[55] These actions which the industry has deemed essential to their survival nevertheless undermine the U.S.-owned domestic production capability vital to national security. These developments inevitably make the mobilization base dependent upon foreign-based suppliers who could prove unreliable in an emergency.

The NMTBA 232 petition is a comprehensive analysis of the industry and its role in a mobilization contingency.

---

[55]U.S. Department of Commerce, 1987 U.S. Industrial Outlook, Washington, D.C., p. 21-1.

The petition provides valuable data and analysis not found elsewhere on how vital machine tools are to mobilization and how the degradation of the industry through imports has affected national security. The NMTBA approach could easily serve as an analytical model for assessing the status of all endangered industry sectors. This type of analysis should be a requisite addendum to more detailed mobilization preparedness planning with each of the "strategic industries". It could provide a reliable assessment of their supply capacity in an emergency-mobilization context. Once compiled, the information should be incorporated into our national security strategy so that assessments of wartime strategy are predicated upon an accurate capability appraisal. It would also provide policy makers with a rationale for programmatic initiatives to improve the responsiveness of these industries. NMTBA, one of the relatively few organizations that has engaged in such a comprehensive exercise, provides an excellent case study of analytical procedures and findings which are applicable to other basic industries.

In its petition NMTBA sought trade relief in the form of quotas on metal-cutting and metal-forming machine tools imported into the United States. Specifically, the Association requested a five-year regime of quotas limiting imports to 17.5 percent of consumption for both metal-cutting and metal-forming markets. In substantiating its case, the NMTBA provided an analysis which included the following information and argumentation:[56]

1. A thorough description of the machine tool market, its size in terms of shipments, market structure, technological influences and macroeconomic determinants.

2. A case-supporting statement of U.S. national security industrial policy, citing laws and precedents established to protect vital industries threatened by imports. This includes reference to the National Security clause of the Trade Agreements Act of 1954 which limits the President's ability to reduce tariffs on goods if such a reduction would threaten domestic capacity needed for defense requirements. Subsequent amendments to the clause have strengthened the Presidents ability to protect strategic industries.

---

[56]National Machine Tool Builders Association, McLean Va.

3. How the National Security clause affirms a general national policy to conduct the affairs of government in peacetime so that the nation will be prepared to meet a military emergency and is consistent with international law and trade provisions.

4. A statement of the critical importance of machine tools to our national security and conventional deterrent posture, expanding on their role in mobilization and describing how bottlenecks in war materiel production during the Korean conflict were attributable to machine tool supply shortages. As noted earlier, under any scenario it must be assumed that machine tool demand would grow precipitously. Given the Soviet nuclear capability and recent arms control trends, the likelihood of a protracted conventional conflict has increased while the credibility of the nuclear "option" has diminished.

5. An examination of how import penetration of the domestic market threatens to impair national security. Analysis of economic data shows a depressed domestic industry. The document cites trends in new orders, shipments (real and nominal), employment, capacity utilization, profits and capital investment including R&D. Future downward trends for the industry are forecast.

6. A demonstration that in a national emergency, the U.S. could not rely upon foreign-based suppliers. Foreign governments would have to satisfy their own requirements before supplying the U.S. market, and certain strategic realities such as geography in the case of Japan present other problems.

7. Realistic defense production scenarios were used to estimate derived demand for categories of machine tools. When demand and supply estimates were compared under widely accepted contingency assumptions, the availability of machine tools was inadequate for support of emergency defense requirements.[57] Furthermore, it was found that the Machine Tool Reserve is obsolete and that the trigger program is not effective. (The Machine Tool Reserve is a program designed to stockpile a production capacity in case of a national emergency and trigger orders are supposed to

---

[57]See Chart 7, Appendix A.

specify in advance the supply requirements of a particular producer should an emergency be declared as a means of mobilizing the machine tool industry).

8. A review of existing civilian machine tool inventories and prospects for their conversion for defense needs had a negative result. Most civilian machine tools are obsolescent or too specialized for defense purposes, and conversion would not work.

9. The overall finding of the petition was that the imposition of restrictive quotas on imports of machine tools would reduce the threat to national security by increasing the domestic production base. NMTBA provided a detailed graphic analysis of how quotas would affect the domestic market and what the impact on supply would be should a national emergency be declared with and without the quotas. The analysis provided three different demand and supply schedules based on assumptions of: large conventional war; limited engagement; or no conflict at all.

10. The petition argued that relief would not have dire economic cost consequences to the nation and noted that the industry is dedicated to self-examination and the correcting of deficiencies in management and strategic and production planning, to improve efficiency and competitiveness.

Report Conclusions

NMTBA found that the domestic machine tool industry has been undermined by the recent surge of imports. Imports have grown from a 16.5 percent share of the U.S. market in 1977 to 27 percent in 1982 measured in value terms.[58] (Subsequently, they increased to a 49 percent share for 1986). Since the report was written, the situation for the industry has further deteriorated significantly. Most of its vital statistics have depreciated in the order of 20-30 percent,[59] and it is argued that the threat to national security has increased proportionately. The threat can be measured by the degree to which mobilization would be delayed by the inadequate production capacity of the

---

[58]NMTBA. See Chart 8, Appendix A.

[59]NMTBA, Economic Handbook, 1986-1987.

42

domestic machine tool industry, predicated upon strategic planning contingencies. The implications of an inadequate machine tool production capability are historically evident; moreover, NMTBA's analysis shows that the projected discrepancy between demand and supply in the event of a major conventional war is becoming more pronounced.

The nature of the next war and sophisticated weapons systems are likely to exacerbate the surge-mobilization problem. A shorter lead-time is probable and the complicated demands on defense-related machine tools are likely to place severe limitations on production even in an emergency when resources could be diverted and focused. A less tangible problem is the manpower shortage. The machine tools industry requires a relatively experienced labor pool to operate efficiently. As people leave the industry while few young people commit themselves to what is perceived as a dying vocation, the U.S. knowledge and experience resource is being depleted. The shortage of critical labor skills would be a difficult constraint to overcome should a national emergency be declared.

Action on the 232 petition

After lengthy bureaucratic iterations, the President finally agreed with the the Department of Commerce findings that the machine tool industry had indeed deteriorated to the extent that national security was impaired. By statute the President is required to consider action; but no stipulation is placed on how and when he should respond. In keeping with the current administration's policy of a non-confrontational approach to trade issues, the President sought voluntary restraint agreements (VRAs) from the major competing nations. Japan, Taiwan, West Germany and Switzerland agreed to place limitations on their exports to the U.S. In most cases the agreement is to cap U.S. domestic market-share penetration of high-tech machine tools at 1981 levels for Japan and Taiwan, and at 1985 levels for West Germany and Switzerland.[60] It is still to early to judge results of the VRA's.

The President has also initiated a machine tool action plan which calls for among other things:

---

[60]U.S. Department of Commerce, "Statement by Secretary of Commerce Malcolm Baldridge", Washington, D.C., December 16, 1986.

1) Greater coordination between DOD and the machine tool industry.

2) DOD-sponsored research to benefit the industry in a civilian as well as military capacity. The DOD Manufacturing Technology Program ("Mantech") has designated the machine tool industry a "thrust area" i.e. a major subject of focus. DOD will be responsible for administering and coordinating this program which will focus on technologies with broad commercial application as well as developments which provide material benefits to DOD.

3) The creation of the National Center for Manufacturing Science as a focal point for machine tool and manufacturing companies to pool scarce R&D resources. The Federal government has committed 5 million dollars a year during the next three years in matching funds for the center.

Outlook

An excess world gross capacity for machine tool production portends stiff competition for years to come.[61] In order to compete, the U.S. industry must become far more efficient and use new technological capabilities to develop market potential and to enhance productivity and design. The marketing trend is towards production systems whereby machine tool manufacturers are contracted to develop and manage production from raw material to finished product. The steps taken by the administration through the machine tool action plan are at best long-term contributions to current competitiveness problems. With the assimilation of high-technology design and control into the industry, the action plan should eventually enable U.S. producers to enhance market positions in a segment with major growth potential. Flexible manufacturing and robotics industries could buttress but not supplant domestic machine tool production capacity. Advances in these sectors should not be seen as alternatives to machine tool products, since machine tools are vital components to these industries as well. In the interim, the trend will be towards internationalization with foreign firms moving to circumvent the export restrictions by developing a U.S. production

---

[61]See Chart 9, Appendix A.

capability. If anything, the U.S. initiative on VRAs and pending trade legislation could exacerbate this trend.[62]

Some observers believe that the industry could possibly decline another 50 percent from the 1986 level before stabilizing. This dramatic deterioration from what is already considered a dangerously low level of capacity should present a major worry for national security mobilization planners. The analysis done by NMTBA in 1983 graphically depicted the shortcomings that existed in supply to meet a national security emergency. Given that the industry may decline still further, possibly by 70 percent from the 1983 assumptions, what was considered a national security threat can only be viewed now as a near crisis.

The machine tool industry represents a clearly vital sector for defense production that is demonstrably vulnerable in terms of international competitiveness. It provides a prototypal case for analytical modeling and programmatic intervention as discussed above. Some effective short-term and long-term measures have been taken to realign supply and demand balances for emergency purposes. But a compelling need remains to evolve and implement a comprehensive defense industrial strategy to secure the position of the especially vital machine tool sector.

---

[62]U.S. Department of Commerce, 1987 U.S. Industrial Outlook, p. 21-3.

E. Semiconductors

As a leading-edge high technology sector, the semiconductor industry has made widespread contributions to defense and civil components of the U.S. economy. While it is still young, it is nonetheless confronted with many problems similar to those of more mature industries associated with defense mobilization. Given the preponderant Soviet conventional force structure, the U.S. will rely increasingly upon technologically superior armaments to maintain a credible conventional deterrent.

Electronic components are crucial to enhancing systems capability and maintaining a technological advantage over the quantitatively superior Soviet forces by upgrading performance as well as maximizing the effectiveness of weapons application. Semiconductors are the building blocks of the latest electronics and their application to defense systems has grown precipitously over the years. While semiconductors are vital to defense, military end use in peacetime represents less than 15 percent of the industry's output by value. In order to have a viable domestic supply, it is imperative that the industry be able to compete globally. Recognizing the need to maintain a healthy semiconductor industry for national security purposes, the Department of Defense commissioned a Defense Science Board study group chaired by Norman Augustine, CEO of Martin Marietta, that examined the impact of foreign source dependency on the U.S. military.[63] This case study is a summary of the group's findings.

Data complications make a full exploration difficult. The industry is divided into "captive" and "merchant" sectors, with the captive supplier being a division of a larger corporation and tied to a vertical demand network. Thus industry data is not explicitly reported for the semiconductor-producing segment but for the corporation as a whole, which makes determining actual semiconductor capacity for captive suppliers difficult to access. It remains unknown whether this capacity could be converted for national security purposes in the event of a national emergency. Another statistical ambiguity is the way in

---

[63]Defense Science Board. "Report of Defense Science Board Task Force on Defense Semiconductor Dependency", Office of the Under Secretary for Acquisition, Department of Defense, Washington, D.C., February 1987.

which foreign penetration of the respective markets (U.S., Japanese) is reported. There is a tendency to under-report the foreign penetration in the U.S. market. The U.S. defines domestic capacity as including all facilities which produce in the U.S. regardless of ownership. The Japanese include only domestically-owned capacity in their statistics. Thus, all production by U.S.-owned facilities based in Japan are considered imports while the production by Japanese-owned facilities in the U.S. are considered domestic facilities and not accounted for in U.S. trade statistics. The extent of foreign penetration and possible control of the U.S. market is therefore far greater than government trade figures indicate. Any evaluation of domestic capacity must take into account Japanese owned domestic facilities which might not prove reliable or responsive in a national emergency. (This general question is explored elsewhere in the paper.)

Few industries bear on U.S. war materiel production capability as directly as the semiconductor industry. Semiconductor "chips" are sold as a commodity and serve as components in almost every major weapons system developed in the past decade. While maintaining strong and steady growth the U.S. industry has long since lost its preeminent international position. The Japanese have shown continued growth since 1975 and if current trends continue they could place the U.S. capacity in jeopardy. Another aspect of the problem of growing foreign-source dependency is the degree to which domestic producers rely upon offshore facilities for various stages of semiconductor production. Typically, many labor-intensive operations of the semiconductor production cycle are performed overseas while research, design and development remain onshore.[64] Thus, while these resources are considered part of the domestic capacity their availability during a national emergency remains problematic. Also, the production equipment and field engineering support base for semiconductor production has become highly

---

[64]"Over 80 percent of the U.S.-based semiconductor assembly is performed offshore"; Warren E. Davis and Daryl Hatano, "The American Semiconductor Industry and the Ascendancy of East Asia", California Management Review, 1985, p. 129. See also Air Force Magazine, where an editorial outlines the semiconductor question and concludes: "The worst part of the problem may be that we do not yet know how bad it is."

competitive in recent years, resulting in growing foreign dependency by U.S. firms.

According to the Defense Science Board, the viability of the semiconductor industry is being threatened by the inability of U.S. industries to compete in commercial (high volume) production sectors. The dynamic random-access memories (DRAMs) represent the benchmark semiconductor chip as "they are the most challenging to manufacture competitively and their development establishes the pace for progress in semiconductor technology". Greater economies of scale and more efficient production have created major price reductions for DRAM's, while production has moved offshore and is currently dominated by the Japanese. Many higher end-product industries have followed the semiconductor trend and are establishing facilities for offshore production. This undermines U.S. capacity in computers and peripheral equipment. Semiconductor design and development are primarily American dominated. The U.S. also has a tenable advantage in the production of specialty chips, which essentially fill niches left by mass production and are profitable at relatively low volumes.

Technological and manufacturing superiority requires a strongly competitive and dynamic mass production capability. The lag in achieving available production efficiencies inhibits capital and R&D investment and in essence dooms the domestic supply to a second-class status. Capital and technological resources are more likely to flow to Japan and other East Asian countries where the perceived competitive advantage lies. Offshore production may place the semiconductor supplier industries in jeopardy as well. Equipment and materials supplied to semiconductor producers must maintain a high level of sophistication and development.

As production moves offshore, the domestic equipment industry will deteriorate, making domestic semiconductor producers dependent upon foreign suppliers for the latest equipment. The U.S. possesses substantial resources at the captive segment of the market where chip production is used to facilitate vertical demand within the corporation (e.g. IBM, ATT). These firms could find themselves under increasing domestic supplier constraints as the merchant segment continues to be undermined by low cost Japanese imports. Thus, while it is not clear where the viability threshold exists, the lack of critical mass for development and economy of scale for competitive position may gradually offset the captive producer base which is predicated on proprietary control of selective technologies. The inability of U.S. producers to compete across the entire spectrum places the industry as well as suppliers to the

48

industry in future jeopardy. Merely satisfying the specialty segment is not enough to safeguard the industry, and recent trends in that part of the market indicate a growing Japanese influence.

According to the Defense Science Board, the U.S. share of the worldwide merchant semiconductor market has declined steadily from approximately 60 percent in 1975 to 49 percent in 1985. Japan's market share has grown precipitously in the same period from 20 percent in 1975 to 40 percent in 1985, and it surpassed the U.S. in 1986. For the DRAM sector, the Japanese have eclipsed U.S. producers as the U.S. market share has declined from 100 percent in 1975 to less than 5 percent in 1985 for merchant producers.[65]

Industry Structure

It is important to consider differences in industrial structure when evaluating competitive disposition. The Japanese "merchant" producers are predominantly segments of larger corporations and thus have a "captive" market as well. This provides obvious cost benefits and economies of scale unavailable to U.S. merchant market producers who are for the most part dependent upon the vagaries of the commodity structure. It also allows for subsidy across product lines for supporting research, achieving advanced development and implementing superior manufacturing processes.

For most Japanese firms, semiconductors account for 5-22 percent of sales whereas U.S. producers rely upon chips for over 50 percent of sales. In terms of overall size, U.S. firms range from $900 million to $5.7 billion while the Japanese range is $1.6 billion to $18 billion.[66] The Japanese firms are therefore better oriented to deal with structural downturns that are inherent to any market and are able to supply consistent resources to R&D so vital to an industry where a state of the art generation is 2.5 years. Domestic industries, on the other hand, are vulnerable to economic shocks as the past few years potently demonstrate. The shocks have long-term consequences as the industry is forced to cut back on investment, which disrupts future development and competitiveness.

---

[65]Defense Science Board. See Chart 10, Appendix A.

[66]Bro Uttal. "Who Will Survive the Microchip Shakeout", Fortune, January 6, 1986. p. 82.

The implications to national security are clear enough. Japanese semiconductor producers are obligated to supply the needs of their vertical sister companies. Should a national emergency be declared in our country, a foreign source could not be guaranteed. In certain specialty markets, the Japanese advantage is such that should the supply be cut off the U.S. would be faced with a severe shortfall in production capability. For instance, the Japanese share of the world ceramic packaging market segment is 95 percent and most of the domestic suppliers either distribute Japanese produced products or depend upon Japanese hardware for their production.[67]

Ceramic packaging of semiconductors is essential to armaments in order to assure reliability, especially under battlefield conditions. Within a mobilization scenario it is doubtful whether the present U.S. semiconductor industry capability is adequate to satisfy emergency demand. Even in a nonemergency contingency, the Japanese firm would have a tremendous incentive to withhold state of the art technology from the U.S. market in order to allow higher value-added Japanese computer manufacturers to gain a competitive advantage.

According to the Defense Science Board Task Force the Japanese also have cost advantages over the U.S., including lower cost of capital. U.S. real interest rates are considerably higher than the Japanese equivalent and profitability expectations here are much higher. In the U.S. a firm must achieve greater results in a shorter period of time often at the expense of long term viability. Industry structure is another factor. Virtually all Japanese firms which sell semiconductors are larger and far more diversified (both horizontally and vertically) than their U.S. counterparts.

Outlook

Shipments for the industry are expected to grow at a rate of 11 percent annually through the 1990s as the industry continues to outpace the 2.7 percent annual growth

---

[67]"Materials and Packaging Systems", Electronic News, August 17, 1987.

predicted for real national product.[68] Employment growth is expected to exceed the national average for non-agricultural employment as well. Market share statistics are difficult to gage as the appreciating yen has a strong impact on the semiconductor market which is commodity-like in structure. Other nations, especially the newly-industrialized East Asian countries such as South Korea and Taiwan have adjusted their strategy to take advantage of perceived opportunities as their currencies remain relatively stable vis-a-vis the dollar. Japanese corporate strategy tends to emphasize the importance of market share, and the Japanese semiconductor producers may be willing to absorb losses or low rates of return rather than lose market share.

Paradoxically, the best opportunity for growth lies in the newly-industrialized countries (NICs) to which many of the producers of higher end products have moved their production facilities. The Japanese have found such invest- ment propitious as the yen strengthens, and the governments of the NICs are working hard to coordinate policies with the indigenous private sector in order to maximize gains.

The U.S. on the other hand has placed greater emphasis on managing cost in its procurement practices, which has further debilitated domestic capacity by stimulating U.S. suppliers to purchase from lower-cost producers overseas. For the U.S. this means that the best market opportunities lie in those countries among our trading partners which are presently the least hospitable to "fair" trade. Thus the imperative will be placed on loosening trade restrictions, especially tariff and non-import barriers, to enable U.S. semiconductor producers to compete fairly. Given the size of the U.S. market and the degree to which these countries are dependent upon U.S. consumption, ample leverage exists by applying principles of reciprocity to effect positive opportunities for U.S. producers. But whether the political will exists to alter past practices allowing unilateral advantage remains problematic.

Technological trends do not bode well for domestic U.S. producers as the Japanese continue to advance and surpass U.S. capabilities in many subsectors of semiconductor production.[69]

---

[68]Department of Commerce, 1987 U.S. Industrial Outlook, Washington, D.C., 1987.

[69]See Chart 11, Appendix A.

51

The reasons for this continuing U.S. technological malaise as outlined by the Task Force include: "lower productivity, demand for a higher wage base, occasional lower standards of quality, an adversarial relationship among management, labor, academia and government, and neglect of the technical manpower base".[70]

Academic standards and engineering practices have fostered a technologically literate society in Japan where employees are trained to develop a comprehensive expertise on a subject or technique as opposed to the generalized knowledge found amongst American workers. This is particularly true for the production technologies where the U.S. is facing an ever-diminishing competitive posture. Attracting people to an industry where much of the production occurs offshore is difficult. There is little incentive for college-bound engineers and technicians to invest years of study (not to mention thousands of dollars) in a field where little or no domestic industrial base exists. It is perhaps in the human resources sector that the U.S. semiconductor manufacturers must find the solution to the pervasive problem of replicating the production quality and reliability of Japan and other competitors.

The U.S. lag in production technology is growing as expertise in this country diminishes owing to domestic procurement of offshore supplies. Initially, U.S. products were licensed to overseas producers where the semiconductors were produced less expensively and more efficiently and by transferring technical and managerial know-how to foreign locations. This practice undermined the U.S. production capability by inhibiting capital investment in production technology. Industry experts have now discovered that offshore production especially in third world countries has eclipsed U.S. technological capabilities to the point where in some cases, U.S. producers are unable to duplicate some production processes. The trend is towards continued obsolescence of U.S. mass production capabilities as technological resources and expertise move offshore. The residual effect on semiconductor industry equipment suppliers is profound. The trend seems to dictate a depletion of the equipment industry at an ever-increasing rate as semiconductor production continues to lag.

---

[70]"Report of the Defense Science Board Task Force on Semiconductor Dependency", p. 9.

Task Force Recommendations

The Task Force came to the conclusion that the U.S. will depend largely upon foreign-based sources for semiconductor hardware and technology unless positive actions are taken to revive U.S. manufacturing capability. The principal steps suggested by the Task Force include:

1) Establishment of a Semiconductor Manufacturing Technology Institute (SEMATECH). A public-private venture for improving the manufacturing base. The facility would serve a quasi-captive function as a principal supplier to DOD. The resources are to be provided by a consortium of industry leaders and the government to the tune of $500 million per year. This very promising project is only in the early stages of implementation but may have substantial potential.

2) Setting up centers of excellence for semiconductor science and engineering at eight universities.

3) Increasing DOD spending for research and development in semiconductor materials, devices, and manufacturing infrastructure.

Clearly, the Task Force and the DOD have recognized the fundamental structural problem within the semiconductor industry. While the industry remains statistically viable, industry and market trends do not bode well for U.S. competitive capacity. In the context of domestic viability, unchecked growth in dependence on foreign production could make producers of higher-end products vulnerable to technological coercion i.e. foreign sources should withhold state-of-the-art products from U.S. markets.

In a national security context, the U.S. could find itself cut off in an emergency situation where mobilization is critical and mass production capabilities are severely depleted. For certain components such as ceramic packaging, the U.S. is already dangerously dependent upon Japanese capacity. The opportunity still exists for rectification of many of these structural problems before the industry yields to the hopelessness that has affected many basic industry sectors. A coordinated government and private effort should help to recapture a strong competitive position and ensure a viable surge-mobilization capability.

53

Unlike older basic industries with leadership experience in mobilization efforts, the semiconductor industry has not been schooled in the realities of surge, expansion and conversion for a national security emergency. Given the dynamic competitive environment of the semiconductor industry and the expanding application its product in defense systems, it is imperative that the U.S. evolve a strategy for maintaining technological leadership and viable competitiveness and develop detailed contingency plans for assuring the performance of this strategic sector in an emergency.

Case Study Conclusions

In the absence of a comprehensive data base and refined analytical models it is necessary to examine the recurring causes of domestic industry sector and subsector malaise in order to prescribe solutions. These illustrative case studies may not be applicable to all key industries, but they seem the best available vehicle for exploring relevant dimensions of the issue.

It is important to consider the cases in the context of overall U.S. manufacturing capability. The deterioration of a particular sector often affects other producer industries. For example the structural concentration of industries is a common phenomenon in maturing sectors, which destabilizes the underlying economic viability and interdependence as these firms deteriorate and capacity wanes. Thus, the implications of a moribund machine tool industry as a vital manufacturing production element are overshadowed by the damage to the economy as a whole. In a national security context, the inability to produce machine tools and spare parts could halt most war materiel production, creating a precarious situation for strategic planners.

Significant common findings on the sectoral case studies include:

1) A general decline, reflected in the available economic and financial statistics.

2) Diminishing domestic market share from import penetration and a growing dependence upon foreign sector and subsector capacity, to the extent that, should a national emergency be declared, redirecting U.S. exports for domestic consumption would not be enough to sustain demand and a serious supply shortfall would be inevitable.

3) Deteriorating profits and capacity as well as a sense of diminishing potential to succeed are reflected in lackluster capital expenditures and R&D efforts.

4) The skilled labor base which is essential to maintaining or regaining capacity is being depleted and there is little incentive for young people to enter what are perceived as dying industries.

5) The general decline of subsectors which depend upon these industries as their primary market.

55

The inability to compete domestically and in the global forum stems largely from application engineering and manufacturing deficiencies and not from a lack of innovation and design. The U.S. is a leader in research and development with some of the most advanced scientific facilities in the world. The breakdown occurs in mass production where competitive prowess means producing goods most efficiently at the lowest cost. Historically, the U.S. has been able to compete against countries that have lower input costs by achieving higher productivity and better quality goods. In the manufacturing context this advantage no longer exists.

Trends indicate further deterioration of general capacity and viability. In the absence of major reform, these case examples and basic industry in general will continue to degenerate under the heavy burden of import saturation. The implications to the overall manufacturing economy are troublesome as foreign-source dependency could place supply constraints, especially for state-of-the-art equipment, on domestic consumers. The significance for national security is clear, since any emergency will have to be addressed by reduced domestic production capabilities. If present trends continue, let alone accelerate, mobilization will cease to be as an important national security option.

The case studies suggest the problems and trends are shared among basic input sectors (raw materials and energy), processing and manufacturing industries (ferroalloys and machine tools) and also higher technology applications (semiconductors). What can be done about them will be explored in Sections IV, V and VI.[71]

---

[71]For an overall assessment of the current status and long term outlook for case study industries see Chart 12, Appendix A.

IV Alerting National Security Policy Makers to Economic Industrial Problems

The industrial base provides the flow of product needed to build force structure, provide for readiness of the force, deploy units, and support logistical requirements during operational phases of a national security emergency. The planning, programming and budgeting system (PPBS) of the Department of Defense (DOD) provides an effective mechanism for determining peacetime defense requirements, budgetary support, and programmable actions needed to carry out the national security strategy and related defense plans—insofar as the currently postured military establishment is concerned.

The adequacy of the U.S. defense industry to support these ends is supposed to be assured by the Five-Year Defense Plan (FYDP) which has stabilized the flow of financial resources through the procurement system to the industrial base. This peacetime resource allocation practice modality has created a "captive defense industrial base" characterized by a few large contractors dominating the competition for major weapons systems and other acquisition programs. In addition, a network of smaller producers operating in a highly competitive derived market environment provides the flow of commodities, components and services needed to maintain the tempo of peacetime activity. Thus, the market structure for major defense programs has evolved into an oligopoly supply side and a monopsony demand side competitive relationship.

This means that most of the requirements for defense in peacetime are met by a captive and specially organized industrial base in which specialized producers provide major weapons systems and support. They in turn rely on a network of secondary and tertiary suppliers for component parts, materiel and raw material inputs. In general, the market relationship linking DOD to its network of industrial suppliers may be properly described as stable and relatively predictable: procurement processes are governed by a well-codified set of regulations appropriate to its market characteristics.

However, the ability of this unique structure to expand to meet the surge requirements in a range of probable national security emergencies is unknown, for much of this arrangement has evolved during a period of reliance on strategic nuclear forces and mutually assured deterrence as the principal contributors to strategic balance between the U.S. and the U.S.S.R. As both the West and its potential adversaries shift to a greater reliance on conventional forces, questions arise regarding the adequacy of the dedicated defense industrial base to meet emergency requirements. That shift in force orientation, as nuclear parity has forced nuclear weapons into a deterrence or retaliatory role only, will be accelerated if new nuclear arms control regimes come into being.

In the late 1970's, defense planners began to worry about the effects on many defense-critical industry sectors of the industrial transition triggered by such factors as the rapid increase in oil prices, inflation, high interest rates, and the growing penetration of the U.S. and international markets by foreign competitors.

In 1981 the House Armed Services Committee produced "The Ailing Defense Industrial Base: Unready for Crisis", a landmark report that unfortunately did not result in sufficient reforms of either the defense community or economic policy-making to reverse the eroding of defense industrial capabilities.

The willingness of leaders to intervene is inhibited by the influence of free market principles on policy formulation, regulatory decisions, and other activities affecting the industrial environment. Thus despite the convincing portrayal of problems in the defense industrial base, little has actually been accomplished.

A major national security emergency in which the U.S. relied primarily on conventional forces would bring into question the adequacy of the captive industrial base to support a surge in defense requirements or transition to a mobilization footing. The Department of Defense, responding to the need to assure production to support conventional force contingencies, has conducted selective surveys of current defense producers to determine their capabilities to respond to emergency requirements and present mobilization plans. These surveys involved current defense producers in an estimating process to determine how much production of existing weapons systems can be increased in a specified period.

The so-called 1519 System utilized for this DOD effort generates some useful data regarding perceptions of current producers concerning various surge and mobilization projections. However, that system proceeds on a set of artificial assumptions to determine the elasticity for production expansion in individual organizations. Its weakness is that many prime contractors and providers of commodities to the DOD rely on the same secondary and tertiary producers of components and raw materials. The one-dimensional approach of the 1519 system, together with the lack of a

58

comprehensive matrix for determining total demands on these lower tier producers brings its reliability into question.

It is precisely in the secondary and tertiary supply networks that the greatest erosion has occurred during the U.S. industrial transition of the last decade. Suppliers of basic industrial products, raw materials, minerals and energy inputs have lost much market position to foreign competition in such sectors as strategic minerals, iron and steel, non-ferrous metals, industrial chemicals, and petroleum. In both U.S. and overseas markets, U.S. producers in these industries have experienced greater competition, poor financial performance, and in most cases significant losses of markets, affecting key subcomponent sectors important for a future mobilization or surge.

Similarly, in such intermediate industrial sectors as forgings and castings, machined metal parts, bearings, electronic components, electrical machinery, turbines, and small internal combustion engines, significant U.S. shares of domestic and international markets have been displaced by foreign producers.

Finally, in more advanced product sectors such as shipbuilding, automotive and transportation equipment, aerospace equipment, machine tools, and electronic equipment, there are early signs of erosion of competitive position by U.S. producers likely to lead to significant losses of market share. Even in such sectors as large-scale computers, integrated circuits, telecommunications and advanced materials and composites, the U.S., while holding a substantial technological lead, is experiencing growing competition, and foreign competitors will probably target such industries as a matter of national economic strategy. High technology industries such as communication satellites, fiber optics, large-scale computers, biotechnology and advanced materials, have all been targeted by Japanese and European interests, and are not immune to the possibility of significant erosion.

The competitive environment in which U.S. firms must operate is growing more intense and there is evidence of a "hollowing out" of many basic secondary and tertiary sectors as well as increased competition in more advanced sectors including automotive, aerospace and machine tools, all important for defense. Finally, similar erosions from widening competition in high-tech sectors important for defense are a growing probability. The recent decline in the exchange value of the dollar may help over time. But the so-called "J-Curve" effect of depreciation does not seem to be working as expected, or at least is taking a very long time. This may reflect the fact that currencies of many major trade competitors are pegged to the dollar and decline along with it, while these countries where currencies have appreciated, such as Japan, are absorbing the loss, as mentioned earlier, to keep market share instead of raising their dollar prices.

While anecdotal information abounds in open sources, and is highlighted in the preceding case studies, it is by no means clear from official sources just how serious the hollowing-out process has become for the defense establishment. The Department of Commerce in its annual industrial outlook publication provides little insight into sectorial decline, at the level of detail needed to assess its implications for meeting defense requirements from domestic sources. Special reports by Commerce, Defense, Interior, the Department of Energy and the like do not provide much insight into the dynamics of changing industrial capacity and its potential effect on national security.

The Department of Defense and the Federal Emergency Management Agency (FEMA) under the Defense Production Act of 1950 (DPA) monitor a number of defense procurement industries and have encouraged and funded selected improvements. But very limited funding has been available for building and maintaining an adequate source of weapon systems, commodities, or parts, components and materials needed to support emergency requirements. Furthermore, there is no systematic assessment of how adequate these efforts are at counteracting the erosion of production capabilities outside the purview of current DOD procurement activities.

Limited funding for such investments has been characteristic of the defense establishment for years. Even under Title III of the Defense Production Act, for decades there has been little authority to fund more than a few programs costing in the tens of millions of dollars annually for the maintenance of viable sectors for defense production. It may be concluded from the lack of a comprehensive data base and assessments of industrial capacity that there is a great deal of uncertainty as to the industrial response in a national security emergency characterized by significant increases in demand for conventional forces.

These requirements would first include filling out the U.S. force posture with systems and expendables to meet combat requirements of an overall 1-1/2 war strategy. In addition, the industrial system to support the mobilization, deployment and possible engagement of conventional forces would require a substantial increase in production of systems and commodities needed to equip Reserve forces likely to be activated.

60

Finally, there is the question of the overall industrial capabilities to support contingency requirements beyond those envisioned in current plans, should a national emergency exceed expected duration and levels of activity. This situation would call for substantially greater flows of production over time well beyond scenarios now envisioned.

In summary, the emergency demands that might be placed on the industrial base are likely to have significantly greater impact owing to enhanced emphasis on the conventional force responses. Also, the readiness of the industrial base to meet mobilization and surge production is uncertain for lack of a comprehensive data base and modeling capabilities for forecasting outcomes of competitive trends.

The dynamic contingency planning system utilized by DOD to anticipate threats and capabilities of potential adversaries and provide the appropriate U.S. responses cannot be matched by assessments of the industrial base. The calculus for determining the overall strategic balance between the U.S. and its potential adversaries must include not only accurate measures of comparative force structures and their likely commitments but also a realistic assessment of their supporting resource and industrial systems.

The foregoing suggests that the U.S. owned and based defense industry is likely to prove inadequate to expanded requirements of many of the likelier crisis scenarios. To what extent is foreign-based capacity an acceptable substitute? It is assumed that foreign-owned but U.S.-based firms would be subject to priority and requisition authority for surge and mobilization to the same degree as domestically owned firms; for example that General Electric's recent sale (actually a swap) of its consumer electronic businesses to the French Thomson firm would not affect their availability for conversion to U.S. war production. But this assumption may merit more detailed legal analysis.

Put another way, can Japan and South Korea and other newly industrializing countries be reliably treated as a part of an extended "global" U.S. defense industrial base, as some DOD officials have implied? The answers depend on a wide variety of assumptions: the nature and geographical location of the emergency, the political attitude of the other governments toward the United States in general and toward its policies in the actual or potential conflict, [72]

---

[72]For this purpose one can treat U.S.-owned but
(Footnote Continued)

the willingness and ability of the foreign suppliers to give the U.S. priority in key allocations and, of course, the vulnerability of their lines of communication and transport to the U.S. Such questions should be treated explicitly in U.S. mobilization planning. And where the maintenance of adequate onshore capacity is infeasible and reliance on offshore production necessary, then prudence suggests both government-level agreements and industry-to-industry contractual provisions giving U.S. orders preferential access to suppliers and priority to production in specified conditions. Yet, insofar as the authors are aware, little has been done along these lines, especially in the most critical foreign dependencies of the second and third tier of U.S. defense suppliers.

In addition to the quantitative demands on industry in a national security surge or mobilization effort, it should be noted that perhaps the overriding consideration is the timeliness of such processes.

In any major surge in defense production or mobilization effort involving activation, provisioning and deployment of reserve forces, success will be determined by the balance between demands and responsiveness in the production base, together with the timing for instituting emergency industrial actions. Specifically, if industrial mobilization or surge production is envisioned as a major contributor to deterrence, and if deterrence should fail, to war fighting capability, then the earlier mobilization and surge actions are taken the more likely the chances of an orderly fulfilling of the requirements. If in the early stages of a developing national security emergency, actions are implemented to surge production, the longer lead-times will help in filling stocks of war reserves, fully equipping the force structure, and providing the necessary flow to stabilize supply and demand.

The traditional model used by defense planners in accomplishing this balance is the D to P, or D-Day to

---

(Footnote Continued)
foreign-based firms similarly. U.S. efforts to apply its laws and controls extra-territorially, as in the case of the Soviet gas pipeline, to foreign subsidies of U.S. firms have met with strong resistance on the ground that host country laws take precedence. There, however, those countries had strong policy differences on the merits with the administration. This would be less applicable in the event of a common emergency which threatened the allies involved.

Production concept. This concept assumes that at the early stages of a mobilization, demand will increase rapidly, and supply will eventually expand and build up at a rapid rate until the flow of new production balances with the requirements.

The advantages of initiating an early surge and mobilization plan based on adequate intelligence and "political" warning, as described below, would shorten the time for accomplishing the D to P balance and would reduce, presumably, the need for large wartime reserve stocks of ammunition, petroleum and other expendables. Thus an effective mobilization doctrine should, emphasize early surge and mobilization actions, the preparation and maintenance of a responsive industrial base to include investments in production capacity, and recognition of lead-times in pacing decisions affecting procurement and stockpiling of materials and minerals.

In order to execute timely mobilization and surge actions there needs to be a series of well-defined steps that trigger transitions in the industrial base and yield greater capacity and responsiveness. Potential bottlenecks in the existing defense industrial base should be identified and standby plans developed to break through these limitations on production through special investments or incentives for private firms to maintain quick-response capabilities. A standby contracting and ordering system should also be set up to include special procurement configurations in the form of letter orders (which have been effective in prior U.S. mobilization efforts) so that administrative delays in activating surge and mobilization responses can be minimized. Contingency budgets should be developed and special financing facilities created to assure adequate financing of the efforts, again to minimize bureaucratic and legislative delays.

Finally, presidential emergency powers should be augmented in such a manner that the defense production base can be "turned on" easily by the Chief Executive and other elements of the Executive Branch responsible for expanding production for defense and civil purposes. Thus, FEMA, DOD, and other responsible agencies should develop coordinating mechanisms for allocating resources for defense and civil preparedness functions. This would require, in effect, an industrial equivalent of the Defense Condition System (DEFCON) by which DOD itself increases the combat readiness of its forces from normal peacetime to full alert condition. But it would have to be stretched out over far longer time periods and in more steps than is the case for DEFCONs.

Moreover, these emergency industrial actions should properly mesh with and reinforce the DEFCON actions.

This brings up the question of warning time. Military planners traditionally speak only of strategic and tactical warning, the former being threatening deployments of opposing forces and the latter evidence of their imminent use. Time intervals are conceived of in terms of days or weeks, too short to accomplish very much in industrial mobilization. Once an attack is underway, in Europe for example, most recent NATO supreme commanders have spoken of their conventional defense capability in terms of days before their supplies were exhausted and they would be forced to capitulate or escalate to nuclear weapons use.

Military professionals are understandably conservative. They cannot rely upon enemy intentions even if we were fortunate enough to have good secret intelligence sources--but only upon enemy capabilities and observed deployments or troop movements and related communications traffic. Thus to be prepared as best they can for the worst case--a Pearl Harbor-type attack--they tend to underestimate the far more likely contingencies of a change in perceived intentions i.e. political warning via a protracted period of worsening relations, threats and counterthreats accompanied by extensive maneuvers and mobilization measures, as occurred several times during the height of the Cold War, for example over Berlin--or appears to be occurring with Iran.

During the Berlin crises, U.S. nuclear superiority was sufficient that raising the DEFCON level and alerting the Strategic Air Command was an effective deterrent. But even then President Kennedy found it prudent to signal his determination to fight for West Berlin by sending in additional forces, increasing tank production, and calling up selected reserve units. Today, a nuclear bluff has limited if any credibility; so that conventional augmentation, and surge and mobilization measures seem a more effective signal and deterrent. Are they also provocative in the sense of leading an enemy to preempt in some way? Views differ; but the authors believe that if done in a low-key precautionary way and pursuant to an established and exercised procedure of civilian-type DEFCONs, such steps are less provocative than military-only measures which could appear more threatening to an opponent's forces.

Moreover, stability in a potential crisis might be enhanced by any future arms control regime which thinned out the East-West military confrontation in central Europe and led to restructured forces and doctrines emphasizing defense and more reliable confidence building measures. A realistic industrial mobilization capacity by the West would contribute insurance to any such arms control structure and thus make its risks more acceptable and its benefits more achievable.

Assuming that mobilization actions can be initiated early in the evolution of a national security contingency, as discussed above, the following streams of activity should be undertaken using a GANTT chart-type process or similar network management techniques: A balanced series of parallel and sequential actions including surging defense production; expansion of the existing defense production base; augmentation of the base by creating new dedicated defense producers; conversion of qualified non-defense producers to defense production; phasing down of civilian production; and activation of cooperative production activities with allies. This last-named action is needed to assure balanced, alliance-wide support of the contingency plans. Such international defense enhancement efforts could also draw in friendly non-alliance members. As discussed, standby governmental and commercial arrangements with negotiated priorities would be needed for access to these foreign production bases.

The quantitative and timing dimensions of the processes discussed above must be integrated with existing strategies and defense policies, including the imperative for timely preparation of public opinion. It is important to determine which industrial sectors and subsectors are truly strategic. Presumably, once this delineation has been achieved an overall proactive strategic plan for the revitalization and maintenance of an adequate national security industrial base can be formulated. Such a plan would place in perspective many questions regarding macro domestic and international policies and the industrial evolution of the U.S.. It would help policymakers in their attempt to channel industrial evolution toward support of national security requirements.

The following is a discussion of considerations for determining the class of industries that should be considered as strategic. First, it is necessary to narrow the field of candidate sectors and subsectors and in the process provide a credible rationale for special attention to these sectors to differentiate national security interests from economic concerns. Ideally, by applying available analytical techniques, it should be possible to list strategic industries essential for defense and critical civilian purposes under a broad spectrum of emergencies.

Under existing DOD guidance, industries which are clearly essential for defense production can be identified and both DOD and FEMA have attempted to develop such lists, reflecting specialized needs for war materiel (so called "war stoppers") and prevent the loss of important mineral, processing and component manufacturing capabilities. For a more comprehensive list, it is desirable to take readings from such sources as: the DOD acquisition community, FEMA, representing the overall national resource perspective, and from the private sector including major defense producers and industrial associations whose inputs have been relatively infrequent. Various models of this approach have been developed by industries as part of their petitions for relief under Section 232 of the Trade Expansion Act of 1962.

Candidates for the strategic industry list would then be examined in terms of such factors as the degree of defense orientation, and the extent of import penetration in the U.S. market, and by applying a set of performance criteria to assess future prospects for the industry. Individual sectors would be defined by the Standard Industrial Classification (SIC) at the three, four or five-digit level of SIC detail and industries would be examined in terms of financial performance, structural characteristics, and international competitive position. This detailed analysis would provide a basis for relating performance of major defense producers to industry averages, provide early warning of possible problems for particular firms, and lay the groundwork for active policy measures to improve industrial capabilities.

The screening mechanism described above can be refined by developing a classification index and grouping strategic industries according to a high, moderate or low degree of vulnerability. This index can be enhanced by weighing such factors as percent of defense orientation together with the degree of import penetration experienced in the industry sector. Either specialized reporting systems should be developed by DOD, DOC, FEMA and other national security agencies or standard listings published by the N.A.M, and other specialized industry associations could utilize the criteria of defense orientation and import penetration which together signal the vulnerability of industry sectors.[73] For example, category I, high vulnerability industries, could be defined as those 3 and 4 digit SIC industry sectors[74] having a 15-20 percent defense orientation in peacetime and

---

[73]See Charts 13 and 14, Appendix A.

[74]See Office of Management and Budget, Standard Industrial Classification Manual, 1972, Washington, D.C.

20 to 30 percent of more import penetration as shown in the sources alluded to above and in the Critical Defense Manufacturing Industries list.[75] Also, industries with rapidly deteriorating degrees of import penetration (i.e. over 2 percent per year) should be added to category I. Here it should be noted that losses in market share are often cumulative and tend to build rapidly beyond the 10 percent range.

Another important indicator that should result in the assignment of an industry to category I vulnerability status might be a high degree of concentration which could lead to a hostile domestic takeover, merger or acquisition, or a foreign takeover. In cases where such changes might lead to closure of facilities, divestiture, or diversification away from the line of defense business affecting a large percentage (20 percent plus) of sector or subsector defense production, careful monitoring and intervention should be considered. The recent takeover attempt of Fairchild Industries by Fujitsu and Harris Corp. by an English consortium poses a unique dilemma. Transfer of such strategically important producers to foreign control has the potential for changing a business from defense to commercial products and for altering its technological position.

Such developments should be carefully monitored from a defense industry perspective and evaluated in terms of vulnerability. Perhaps a special reporting system could require an annual assessment of vulnerability status utilizing the methodology described above. Once the industries in this listing have been classified in one of the three categories of vulnerability, it is then possible to refine the status of each industry by applying an Industry Performance Matrix (IPM).[76]

The matrix can be used to determine current performance, and the five-year and ten-year outlook, in terms of performance, and financial, structural and international competitive indicators. To the degree possible standard financial and statistical measures are employed to assure

---

[75]See Chart 15, Appendix A. This listing has been compiled by the Department of Commerce as a means of alerting the national security community regarding industrial sector and subsectors of special importance to defense in peacetime and under emergency conditions.

[76]See Chart 16, Appendix A.

comparability among industrial sectors and data sources. Once evaluated in terms of the Industry Performance Matrix, category I, II or III industries can be ranked according to need for special attention and support by the national security community.

Planners interested in surge, mobilization and other strategic aspects of industry performance would benefit greatly from such a system. Industries in the category I high vulnerability group could be subjected to detailed analysis of their likely performance in supporting defense requirements in peacetime and under emergency conditions. Producers, industry associations, and research organizations might be queried to estimate the capabilities of these industry sectors and to determine bottlenecks and other impediments to performance sufficient to meet defense objectives. Based on these data and the IPM analysis, DOD and other Executive Branch agencies could take corrective actions on generic as well as sectoral problems and even at the level of individual producers.

V Economic Policy Options: Domestic and International

For improving the viability of strategic industry sectors, various policy options are available to government leaders. These approaches include both developmental actions to improve the competitive position and survivability of U.S. firms and defensive measures to counter international pressures causing serious erosion of domestic and international markets for U.S. producers. As such policy interventions represent an active stance on the part of government, they can be controversial, as is reflected in the debate regarding a "national industrial policy" which has been underway in the U.S. since the oil crisis of 1973-74.

The difficulty in building a consensus in support such of government action rests upon the traditional hesitancy of national leaders to take a direct part in directing the flow of investment or managing enterprise functions. Since government involvement often enhances the position of selected producers at the expense of competitors, it is seen as inappropriate government favoritism. Also, interventions affecting cost structures at lower levels in the vertical flow of production tend to adversely affect cost, prices and profits at successively higher levels, distorting the competitive position of many to benefit a few.

Further, on economic efficiency grounds, many critics of industrial policy argue that the government efforts would interfere with the free market, which is the best means for assuring efficient resource allocation in production. Finally, the move to an active industrial policy conflicts with the view that government in a mixed enterprise system should serve as regulator and framer of the general economic environment, but limit its involvement in resource allocation decisions appropriately left to private interests.

Thus, historical, philosophical and practical limits prevent the U.S. government from intervening to enhance prospects for key industries, defense-oriented or not. In contrast, our major industrial competitors in Europe, Japan and many newly-industrialized societies see a direct government role as desirable, if not essential, to their economic development objectives. Contrasted with the arms-length, regulatory government functions of the U.S. are the active government efforts to stimulate industrial development, lower unemployment, improve competitive posture, and preserve national security assets in many competitor nations.

In such countries important defense industries are treated as a unique national asset and often have preferential financing, tax advantages, tied procurement contracts,

R&D funding, and favorable fiscal and monetary measures to assure their viability and competitive success. In the U.K., France, and other European countries, an explicit economic goal is to improve the prospects for domestic arms producers. In such countries as Brazil, Israel, South Korea and Taiwan, even greater emphasis is placed on economic development objectives and enhanced defense capabilities based on arms trade supported by domestic production.

This reality raises policy issues for the U.S. To a considerable extent, a thriving peacetime defense industrial base requires the economies of scale of a large export market, once furnished by extensive U.S. military assistance programs but now cut back. The NATO allies seek a two way street in cooperative armaments programs, while former third world buyers are now exporters. And the "merchants of death" label is still an unpleasant one for U.S. public diplomacy.

In Japan, however, because of its inherent constitutional limitations on arms exports, defense production efforts are limited to the Self-Defense Forces. Therefore, advanced technology projects that are stimulated by defense requirements are often seen in Japan as prototype efforts leading to improving not only defense capabilities but also valuable contributions to commercial applications.

In the cases cited above, the development of a strong and viable defense industry is an explicit national objective to which fiscal, monetary and developmental economic policies are linked and upon which a supporting political consensus has been consistently built. In contrast, the particular role of the U.S. defense industry as a contributor to economic objectives has seldom been emphasized. The defense sector has seldom received special consideration in policy deliberations and in Congress has been subjected to the same regulatory, fiscal, monetary and developmental influences as have other industries.

The U.S. government would enter a new realm of policy if it attempts to improve prospects for strategic industries in support of defense requirements. To succeed in such an endeavor, the overriding consideration must be to build a consensus that a strong defense industrial base is essential to our long-term strategic interests. To accomplish this an energized policy debate is needed within the executive and legislative branches of government to delineate the limits, rules and organizational roles for special intervention actions. Also, comprehensive consensus-building efforts should be initiated by national leaders reflecting the views of organized labor, industry and trade associations, local, State and regional government and private sector interests.

Such an effort would require a clear enunciation of the U.S. national security interest, the threats posed by potential adversaries, and the need for the U.S. to develop and maintain the best possible industrial system to support these inherent defense requirements, especially in the security environment of the nineties and the early 21st century. That era is likely to differ significantly from the recent past.

A major development in the process of building public support for such an effort is the Congressionally mandated National Strategy Policy Statement referred to earlier. It should be issued by the President in conjunction with the annual State of the Union Message and budget presentation to the Congress. This major policy statement regarding U.S. strategy objectives should include a strong case for developing an adequate industrial and resource base for defense purposes.[77] This strategy statement, together with the annual posture review and Annual Report prepared by the Chairman of the Joint Chiefs of Staff and the Secretary of Defense offer other opportunities for linking the defense industrial improvement to national security strategy and plans.

Once these major policy statements have been promulgated, consideration of policy options designed to improve industry's prospects can be undertaken by a wider community. These are some of the possible action categories:

Macroeconomic Fiscal and Monetary Policies - Overall national economic policy should provide consistent incentives for long-term growth and stability of mutual benefit to the economy and the industrial base. Discretionary government actions should create incentives to maintain aggregate demand in the public and private sector sufficient to meet the following goals: real annual growth in GNP of approximately 3 to 4.0 percent; hold unemployment at about 5 percent; and promote price stability with inflation in the CPI contained around 2.5 to 3.5 percent. If such macro growth and stabilization goals can be achieved—and the authors are well aware of the difficulties many administrations have faced in seeking them—then the domestic economic environment should be conducive to

---

[77]Indeed, as noted in the Introduction, the first such statement included some appropriate language; but it remains divorced from resource realities and budgetary decisions.

improved performance of commercial as well as defense industries.

Defense Budget and Procurement- Recognition of the vital interdependence of the resource base of the U.S., strategic industries and other defense interests should receive expression in DOD budget formulation and resource management. The DOD weapons acquisition process utilizing the Defense Systems Acquisition Review (DSARC) should require that all major systems procurement include analysis of the investment needed to assure surge and mobilization capabilities on the part of defense contractors. Reforms of government-industry procurement practices such as those proposed by the Packard Commission on Defense Management should be implemented.

New acquisition programs should be subjected to a "producibility" test to clarify potential trade-offs in terms of cost, performance, and producibility especially relevant to an emergency. Also, fresh managerial approaches to breaking bottlenecks to production; acquiring long-lead time items in early phases of acquisition; and spreading the sourcing of systems as well as component parts and commodities used in production among a wider array of producers could add needed emergency capacity.

The procurement programs of each military department and the policies of the Office of the Secretary of Defense (OSD) should reflect a concern for mobilization by providing sufficient funds for investments in organizational structures and programs to assure preparedness; making essential investments in the industrial base in terms of expansion capabilities for production in emergencies; modernization of the stockpile of strategic and critical materials and significantly increased funding under Title III of the Defense Production Act to stimulate the expansion of the strategic industrial base and enhance its responsiveness. DOD and other executive agencies such as FEMA, Commerce, and Interior should be required to show concern for both peacetime and for emergency performance of the strategic industrial base in all major programs.

Antitrust Exemptions- In order to promote economy of scale in research and development, production processes, and the acceleration of industry growth and development, selected industries important for defense production should be allowed to operate in a concerted fashion beyond the normal constraints of the Sherman Act and other antitrust laws. Such exceptions, for which there are already precedents in the electronics field,[78] would help U.S. firms counter foreign competition more effectively and permit cooperative planning and development efforts in cooperation with relevant government agencies. The establishment of an industry committee seems indicated to advise DOD and other national security agencies when relief from antitrust regulations seems in order to plan an interchange of relevant data on the competitive stands of US firms and to accelerate technological development applications as well as economies of scale and specialization. Such antitrust exemptions, however, must be limited and monitored to prevent collusion from spilling over into the purely commercial markets and thereby upsetting the natural regulatory functions of the free market in assuring efficiency in the use of national resources.

Expanded R&D Support- Through the offices of such federal agencies as the National Academy of Sciences, National Science Foundation, National Laboratories, and various Federally sponsored programs in major US research universities the Federal government should place a special emphasis on R&D relevant to improving the performance and competitive prospects of critical defense industries. This R&D emphasis should encompass not only the research needed for leadership in high technology sectors but should also advance U.S. interests in manufacturing methods, product quality, and industrial management. This effort should include an expanded DOD program to achieve manufacturing technology improvements such as those recently advocated by the National Research Council.[79] Such national R&D efforts if broadly defined could enhance the competitiveness of U.S. industry overall.

Tax and Financial Incentives- Perhaps the most effective policy instrument for improving the U.S. strategic industries would be substantial financial incentives for

_____

[78]Recent antitrust exemptions involving Micro Electronic Corporation and Sematech, and the proposal for a superconductivity consortium represent possible models for gaining a technological lead in other industrial sectors.

[79]Manufacturing Studies Board, Manufacturing Technology: Cornerstone of a Renewed Defense Industrial Base, National Academy Press, Washington, D.C., 1987.

their growth and development. As we have seen, the long-term prospects for such industries are tied to profitability and return on capital and the outlook is not optimistic. Most defense-oriented producers and particularly "captive" ones have been institutionally limited in their profits, return on investment, and return on equity by peacetime procurement regulations and contracting practices.

The result has been cash flow and capital returns insufficient to spur growth and maintain efficiency. When compared to non-defense producers many defense firms are at a disadvantage in terms of access to capital owing to the low rates of return derived from current DOD contracting procedures, and they are adversely affected by the cyclical and uncertain nature of DOD procurement budgets. Recent reforms in U.S. tax treatment of depreciation, investment tax credits, and other contributors to cash flow make it more difficult for defense producers to raise investment capital for modernization and long-term efficiency. Special treatment of designated strategic industries allowing enhanced cash flow and profitability through some combination of reduced tax rates on earnings, special tax credits for capital investments, and special depreciation allowances for capital recovery would all contribute to financial prospects and viability.

Special Financing Facility- A more direct means of aiding U.S. strategic industries would be the creation of a government-supported facility for financing defense operations of essential firms in the defense production base and those that might wish to enter it. The creation of a special defense industry financial facility, perhaps of a government-sponsored industrial development bank, could markedly improve access to capital in peacetime and rapidly provide financial support in emergency conditions. Such a financial institution could be operated with an independent board, utilize appropriate measures of risk in making loans, and derive its capital from the major U.S. money markets, helped by the government's full faith and credit, in much the same manner as other development lending institutions or federal mortgage banks.

Such an approach would be most appropriate in an emergency period when uncertainty and confusion might inhibit the needed flow of capital through traditional channels. In peacetime such an approach would have to be cautiously applied or major opposition would likely develop in commercial banking circles.

Government Subsidy- In cases where industry sectors or major producers are unable to maintain a competitive position, even with improved efficiencies, and where private efforts have been unable to assure the long-term viability of key industrial units, it may be appropriate to introduce subsidies. They could be provided by DOD, FEMA, or a National Security Industry Authority operating in the context of a revitalized National Security Resources Board discussed below.

The use of subsidies in peacetime is of course highly controversial, and it is generally appropriate only in extreme cases where the national interest overrides the market interactions that would otherwise eliminate production in the U.S. Subsidies are used in agriculture, transportation, energy and other industrial cases, despite opposition from the Reagan and other recent Administrations because a subsidized industry escapes some of the normal market forces that affect risk taking and improved efficiency. Subsidies and price guarantees under the Defense Production Act of 1950 as experienced during the Korean war may be the most effective way of strengthening minerals and materials production and other industry sectors vital to an emergency.

Arrangements of this type might be considered if, as expected, the U.S. should lose or be threatened with the loss of a number of key industrial facilities over the next few years in the absence of government intervention. While peacetime subsidies seem an extreme measure, maintaining at least some standby capacity could prove vital in the early stages of a mobilization effort. The key to the effective application of subsidies is the development of analytical capabilities for sorting out the legitimate claimants from the multitude. Also some mechanism for recovery of excess profits that might accrue to subsidized producers, through the application of special taxes or a re-negotiation process would be needed to counteract what might prove to be unnecessary subsidies or to share the benefits of unexpected efficiencies or windfall gains.

Creation of an Arsenal System- If key industrial sectors and major producers should fail to maintain their competitive positions and be in danger of permanent closure, their takeover and inclusion in an expanded defense arsenal system might be considered. Precedents for such systems exist in the cases of ammunition, nuclear weapons, tank production, shipbuilding, and transportations.

In these cases various industrial plants and facilities are either government-owned and operated (GOGO) or

75

government-owned and contractor operated (GOCO). In either case the government provides facilities, covers production cost, and exerts either direct or indirect managerial control. A variant of this system exists in the aerospace, machine tool, and certain other sectors whereby specialized government equipment is provided to private contractors for their use or maintenance during peacetime in order to be available for emergencies. While the performance record of many arsenal-type enterprises has been poor in terms of efficiency, cost, and quality of commodities produced, under emergency conditions an arsenal system would be a useful tool in overcoming capacity deficiencies exist in the private industrial base when operating in a more or less open trading environment.

Trade Intervention- As much of the competitive pressure on U.S. producers in the traditional sectors important for defense mobilization emanates from abroad, there is a need to consider selective trade restrictions to support those industries determined to be essential under evaluation procedures such as those outlined above. Tariffs, quotas, and the negotiation of voluntary restraint agreements (VRA's) are all policy instruments that could protect the competitive positions of key U.S. producers. Such interventions, however, may create undesirable side-effects, such as trade and diplomatic retaliation and reduced domestic production efficiency, both of which penalize U.S. consumers. Their use should therefore be contemplated with great care.

At present, the executive branch has authority under the Trade Expansion Act of 1962 and the Emergency Economic Powers Act to take protection measures in cases affecting national security. With respect to international trade actions, under terms of the General Agreement on Tariffs and Trade (GATT) there is a recognized escape clause provision and precedent that allows nations to make restrictive arrangements to maintain industrial and resource sectors for national security. Therefore, if a program of trade restrictions were implemented, the negative international reaction should be manageable. It would however require the building of a domestic consensus on the need for limited protectionist measures and the initiation of bilateral and multilateral diplomatic efforts with trading partners and international institutions.

If careful analysis of the need for the implementation of trade restrictions were accomplished and clearly justified actions taken only in cases of defense criticality where no other effective alternatives were available, it should be possible to utilize such devices successfully. Private interests often argue the national security rationale, however tenuous, in seeking government protection against legitimate foreign competition. Such tendencies must be guarded against to prevent the exceptions we have in mind from becoming the rule. This reservation is especially relevant given the growing sentiment for protectionism in the face of competition from both established and newly-developed industrial societies. Thus trade restrictions for national security purposes should stand on their own rationale as determined by the government itself, not the interested parties and not become entangled in the larger free trade debate.

Control of Direct Foreign Investment- The accumulation of foreign exchange earnings resulting from highly favorable trade balances with the U.S. by Japan, West European countries, and others provides financial leverage which finds its way into portfolio and direct investment accounts in the U.S.. Given the favorable exchange rates, conversion of currencies of these nations into dollar terms provides a relatively low price for U.S. equities and industrial resources, some cases less than the book value of actual assets.

Foreign investors are increasingly seeking investments in major industrial enterprises although foreign capital remains preponderantly in volatile, portfolio type investments.[80] The principal attractions of such investments are basic industries in the U.S. which have financial difficulties and are finding it difficult to generate capital needed for modernization. These firms find often that foreign investors are eager to enter into equity positions and in some cases are interested in complete takeovers. Since many of the industries in the defense industrial base, particularly suppliers of components and parts, are experiencing such cash flow and earnings difficulties they are especially vulnerable to takeovers by foreigners. These investors are also interested in high technology sectors, presumably with a view to bringing home the latest technology to the capital exporting country. Some greater U.S. government control and

---

[80] R.L. Danielian and S.E. Thomsen, The Forgotten Deficit, International Economic Policy Association, Westview Press, Boulder.

77

strategic direction of these industries may be warranted where foreign acquisition is involved

The United States passively monitors incoming foreign investments through a Treasury-chaired interdepartmental committee called CFIUS (Committee on Foreign Investment in the U.S.) and collects limited statistical data. But approvals are required only where antitrust or securities law apply, as they would be for a purely domestic merger or acquisition. Foreign participation can also be restricted by various specific statutes applying to atomic energy, transportation, and telecommunication. There is also reciprocity legislation on the books limiting certain acquisitions, e.g. public lands, by nationals of countries which do not permit U.S. nationals to invest or own property in their own country. But actual cases are few and the necessary waivers or determinations are usually granted.[81]

The main government recourse against foreign takeovers of key defense firms is a determination by the Defense Department that the firm may not be granted contracts or security clearances under the new management. This deterrent was apparently used effectively in the attempted purchase of Fairchild by Fujitsu. DOD is also monitoring a possible takeover attempt by the T. Boone Pickens group involving Boeing, not because of foreign involvement, but out of concern over the group's lack of experience in aerospace and the possible dimunition of productive assets.

The authors believe that the U.S. should remain open to foreign investment as a matter of basic economic policy. In fact, we need continuing inflows to offset our serious fiscal and balance of payments deficits, even while we strive strive for greater U.S. investment access to our major trading partners. However, for the reasons outlined above, we believe that notification and reporting requirements should be tightened and administrative approvals required where defense-sensitive industries or leading technologies are involved. Most other industrial democracies have such requirements, usually stricter than what is suggested here. This will probably require enactment of

---

[81]A recent case involved a Kuwait merger deal with Santa Fe International Corporation under the Mineral Leasing Act which calls for reciprocal access to mineral resources. It was determined by the Department of Interior that reciprocity was not violated under the terms of the act.

statutory authority by Congress,which has already shown
signs of concern.

Control of Technology Transfer- Although the government
retains the right to control U.S. exports of goods and
technologies under the Export Control Act, the principal
multilateral mechanism for controlling the flow of technology vital to U.S. and Allied security is administered by
a Coordinating Committee (COCOM). This voluntary grouping,
which includes NATO, Japan and other non-NATO countries,
maintains a list of militarily important products and
commodities and tries to prevent them from flowing to the
Soviet Union and other communist nations.
This procedure is effective within its limitations, and
there is a policy consensus supporting denial of strategic
goods; but there are frequent conflicts in national licensing procedures for so-called "dual use" items. For example
an advanced machine tool could be used to make either tanks
or tractors. COCOM attempts to coordinate national policies
and licensing procedures on such matters but has suffered
from disputes between prospective sellers (and their government backers) who stress the economic advantages of East-
West trade and those who give top priority to the strategic
implications.
Recent cases suggest that the system needs strengthening to prevent critical technology leakage to Soviet bloc.
By focusing mainly on finished products, COCOM inadequately
recognizes that the transfer of technology itself, which
generally takes the form of intellectual property, may be of
greater value in the long run to communist defense capabilities. There have been battles between DOD and Commerce,
with the former tending to be more restrictive, as well as
among COCOM members.
The recent emphasis has been on tightening controls on
"critical technologies" while liberalizing restrictions
elsewhere. But the task of identification itself has proved
difficult, and it may be that a new agency is needed. It
could be attached to the NSC at a policy and coordinating
level with actual licensing reviews conducted by Commerce,
Defense and State, as at present, and bring a heightened
awareness of the strategic significance of technology
transfers to potential adversaries, whether through licensing or scientific and scholarly exchanges. In especially
sensitive cases where the national security interest is
potentially involved, even proposed transfers to major
economic competitors might be reviewed and restricted.
Another dimension of technology flow that threatens the
competitive position of strategically important industries

located in the U.S. is industrial espionage. Cases such as the Toshiba-IBM incident raise difficult questions about the limits of legitimate competitive activity and the best means of protecting industrial security. While financial remedies have been forthcoming from the U.S. legal system and guilty parties are called to account for their actions, it is by no means clear that such sanctions are sufficient to deter overzealous competitors.

Another question is whether American diplomatic and counter-intelligence activities are sufficient to deter Eastern bloc countries from acquiring vital technology and production know-how. In both dimensions, efforts must focus not only on specific cases but also on the potential long-range damage to the U.S. defense industrial structure and its capabilities to respond to emergency requirements. Only when national security is factored into the determination of sanctions and financial remedies can the appropriate penalties be assessed. In any event security measures should be tightened and efforts to counter illegitimate moves against the U.S. defense industry enhanced.

Increase Stocks of Strategic and Critical Materials and Minerals and the Strategic Petroleum Reserve— As explained earlier, such stocks are an important hedge against loss of access to foreign sources of raw materials and minerals; and disputes within both the Executive and Congress, largely budgetary, have stymied much needed modernizing of the Defense Stockpile and filling the Strategic Petroleum Reserve.

More aggressive action is clearly needed to break the impasse caused by the ill-fated NSC stockpile goal study described earlier. The subject needs to be treated not in a micro sense but in the macro-strategic context of providing the enhanced mobilization capability for which this study has argued, given the return to an emphasis on conventional forces and sustainability and surge. Rather than reducing the stockpile (except for clearly unneeded surpluses and obsolete items) it should be expanded and upgraded to include more semi-finished materials and even certain critical capital goods. But for this to occur, both public and government attention must be drawn to the relevance of such programs in a time of more ambiguous security threats and budgetary stringency.

When the foregoing actions for strengthening the U.S. defense industrial base are related to measures of vulnerability of industry sectors, subsectors and particular enterprises utilizing criteria described above, it is possible to orchestrate selective interventions to assure the necessary flow in peacetime and emergency conditions. Institutionalization of such an approach together with the building of a consensus for it is a formidable but inescapable challenge.

VI Conclusions and Recommendations

As the new century approaches, the country is being pulled one way by emerging strategic vectors and pushed the other way by economic forces. The result is a growing, if often unacknowledged, tension between its national security and international economic interests.

Nuclear parity or stalemate has brought to the fore the modernization of conventional capabilities, which both the U.S. and its NATO allies are increasingly hard-pressed to provide in the face of sharp political-economic constraints.

A new regime in the Kremlin is equally pressed to modernize its civilian economy and military establishment simultaneously and has displayed an unprecedented "glasnost" (openness) about arms control and arms reductions.

Whether or not this situation ripens into verifiable arms control regimes, the West is being forced by economic factors toward smaller, cheaper, high-quality ready forces backed up by an augmented reserve, surge and mobilization readiness. When this mix is achieved it will be a hedge against unknown future developments and optimize the precise area where the West it is strongest vis a vis the East, namely in industrial and technological prowess.

At the same time rapid technological development and the proliferation of international competitors are inducing major transitions in production and market shares and a growing competition for resources. But for the U.S. and Western Europe and Japan too, the structural changes of a highly competitive world economy are moving away from basic industries and toward service-oriented economies. Tele-communications, financial services and high-speed computers are pacing the way. Despite lapses in practice by many countries (including our own) the principles of free, or at least fair trade are in the ascendency, meaning that market forces and profitability govern trade and investment flows within the context of interdependence. These forces are shifting the world's industrial geography and strategic alignments.

As economists, the authors agree that this trend is desirable from an efficiency perspective, or at least unavoidable, and that the alternatives of protectionism or heavy-handed government "dirigism" are less beneficial for all in the long run--if the world remains relatively peaceful. But the U.S. alone is spending trillions of dollars each decade on the contrary assumption that it may not remain peaceful and that maintenance of a strong military posture is the best guarantee that it will; at least insofar as vital Western interests are concerned.

82

Meanwhile, the desirable peacetime adjustments to structural change are eroding the industrial strength of the military posture the West will need to help maintain that condition! Translating a high-tech civilian economy into a high-tech military posture is neither easy, nor cheap, nor is it always effective ("operable" in Pentagonese). It could be argued that the dilemma postulated by the paper is false, that with greater political will the industrial democracies could eat their butter and have their high-tech guns too, if only they would sacrifice ...welfare... social security... regional development... farm subsidies or whatever offends the particular critic; and in purely economic terms this may be true: after all the U.S. devoted some 40 percent of its GNP to the war effort in the mid-forties, compared to less than 7 percent of a much larger GNP today. But in a climate of established political expectations and "entitlements", it would take a much clearer and more immediate threat to the nation to change its priorities in societal choices between guns and butter. Changing such a traditional peacetime mind-set to a "contingency" mind-set appropriate for new economic and industrial realities in a non-crisis environment, to provide both guns and butter, is unprecedented in U.S. industrial history which has sharply differentiated war and peace.

This paper is an effort to force the basic dilemma to the surface of national awareness. The alternatives are few and stark: steer the present course and wind up with an inadequate or unsustainable conventional military capability; return to an inherently incredible massive retaliation, nuclear-dependent policy, surely a bluff in today's conditions; move towards economic autarchy at whatever cost to the U.S. and world economies; massively increase defense outlays, which is against all the political odds, or adjust our strategic posture to resource reality and moderate our economic policy to maintain the critical elements of an industrial mobilization base to back up a smaller military establishment.

The authors believe that the last-named option is the only prudent and viable one, and they have tried to outline its key components and underlying rationale. To do nothing is to count on either the goodwill or ineptitude of potential adversaries or the low odds of a "master stroke" technological or policy breakthrough for countering threats to national security.

Two additional aspects need to be addressed, at least briefly: costs and organization. We have made no attempt to "cost" the types of policies and actions recommended, and theoretically the sky is the limit, though it should not and cannot be. Rather, our approach has been to assume that the next President takes a zero-based approach to "national security" planning. Do we really need X carrier battle groups, Y air wings and Z active divisions—or Strategic Defense? What could be bought with X (or Y or Z) minus one, or two? On a five-year basis a great deal of readiness, sustainability and surge and mobilization capability could be substituted. This does not take into account other critical components of national security, now nearly starved, such as unconventional warfare capability, public diplomacy, foreign affairs, including human (as opposed to technical) "intelligence", and foreign aid.

This approach rebalances ready capabilities with the assured creation of more robust ingredients in the event of a real crisis. It is beyond the scope of the study to develop a detailed matrix of forces and structures which would permit direct funding of a program for revitalizing the defense industrial base. Nonetheless it would be possible to improve the base substantially with a commitment of one half to 1 percent of the annual defense budget over a period of 10 years. These funds should be utilized to maximize incentives for joint public-private actions such as those proposed in this study.

If the current fiscal and financial crises compels the government to raise additional revenue—such as by a value-added tax--the proceeds could be mandated primarily for deficit reduction, but with a small part also earmarked to meet national security deficiencies, such as those discussed here. In any case, at least the minimum essential funds should become available once new priorities are established. In reality it is the vision of the President that can and should make the tradeoff between current and future risks and benefits in national security priorities.

On the assumption that this will be the case, how can the U.S. structure the resource-reality element into its policy-making machinery? The Pentagon is too riven by service, functional and mission rivalries to be an effective single focus—although of course it must play the key role, albeit with improved defense industry management authority, and capabilities including more qualified personnel. FEMA has capabilities which should be expanded and better utilized, but it is currently too small and too far-removed from the locus of policy to be the lead agency. State, Treasury and Commerce are likewise too preoccupied with their own particular trees to see the whole forest. One option sometimes mentioned is to create a special body, such as a reinvigorated Emergency Mobilization Preparedness Board (EMPB) within the NSC structure itself. But the EMPB, the most recent attempt at such reform, never really got off the ground even in its most active period. At this writing, it is largely inactive or fragmented into low level staff groups owing to the lack of resources, budgetary authority and priorities for mobilization (which OMB has traditionally opposed) and the day-to-day "fire brigade" preoccupations of the Council and its senior staff.

One is therefore forced to the unoriginal suggestion of going back forty years to create a modern version of the National Security Resources Board (NSRB) established in the National Security Act of 1947. In addition to creating the NSC, the CIA and Department of Defense, the Act gave the NSRB the mission of advising "the President concerning the coordination of military, industrial, and civilian mobilization, including programs for the effective use in time of war of the Nation's natural and industrial resources for military and civilian needs... the relationship between potential supplies of and potential requirements for, manpower, resources, and productive facilities in time of war; together with policies for establishing adequate reserves of strategic and critical material" and industrial preparedness and mobilization planning during peacetime. The overall direction of this process represents a formidable challenge in policy formulation and management.[82]

A modern version would have to refer to national emergency or preparedness alerts declared by the President, rather than "in time of war". And the new Board's charter should specify chairmanship by the President or Vice President and membership by the claimant and resource agencies of the executive branch. Most important, the mission should include analyses and recommendations on the linkages of strategy, budgets and industrial mobilization, now handled inadequately by the Defense, OMB and the NSC.

Such a reorganization will be especially critical during the early phase of the next administration which will confront the legacy of a strategy that the politically available resources can no longer support, and a force structure which is not tailored to the likeliest contingencies (as pointed out earlier) and does not provide the requisite staying power in terms of equipment, deployability, sustainability, logistical support and industrial base, let alone a rapid surge or augmentation capacity. Even after new policies, strategies and programs have been

---

[82]See Chart 17, Appendix A.

developed, taking into account the possibility for significant nuclear and conventional arms accords with the U.S.S.R.
over and above the now probable INF agreement, constant
monitoring and adjustments will be required. They should
include the tracking of trends in, and forecasts for, the
critical defense industries as outlined earlier. The goal
of this effort, then, should be the realization of a
dynamic, senior-level policy formulation capability for
balancing strategy and resources within a rapidly changing
international security environment.

The authors see the new body as working in tandem with
the NSC and operating with senior executive leadership and a
small policy staff. The existing Federal Emergency Preparedness Agency (FEMA) should be upgraded and expanded, to
serve as the interagency focal point and coordinator of the
policy direction hammered out in the Board, in cooperation
with the NSC. In wartime or all-out mobilization FEMA's
role should be expanded to make it in fact the senior
operating agency responsible for allocation of national
resources and for coordinating allied efforts in this
regard. (The existing National Critical Materials Council
could be integrated with the new body, since its primary
focus on materials is really a subset of the broader preparedness and mobilization problem the Board would address;
or it could continue independently with its own important
agenda, and assume the lead coordinating role with respect
to critical materials.)

The broad dilemma of resources versus requirements in a
new strategic environment outlined in this paper may be
viewed either as a problem which will simply overwhelm the
next administration and require draconian and wasteful
cutbacks, or as an opportunity to be grasped and turned to
advantage. The authors favor the latter.

Recommendations

(1) Take a new look at the whole range of options for
linking policy, strategy, forces and resources in their
optimum forms in the new strategic environment to the year
2000.

(2) Develop, as one such option, a new set of priorities
with regard to sustainability, surge, rapid augmentation by
ready reserves, and mobilization and thereby counteract the
hollowing out of U.S. defense industry.

(3) Establish an organization parallel to the NSC with a
clear, mandate from the President to participate in the

overall policy review in (1) above and then to develop, coordinate and implement in a cost-effective manner the priorities outlined in (2).

(4) Undertake a formalized review of national security strategies, defense programs and major policy options to determine strategic resource implications and impacts on defense production capabilities.

(5) Require a disciplined, closed-loop interaction between the security program agencies, such as defense with its five-year PPB cycle, and the resource-knowledgeable agencies such as Treasury, Commerce, Interior and FEMA for the purpose of assuring consistency among them in contingency planning and emergency programs with the planning efforts of DOD.

(6) Prepare a classified report to the President assessing the strategic economic position to the U.S. including long-term assessments of macroeconomic trends, competitiveness, productivity, trade position and outlook for key industries and publish an unclassified report similar to those once issued by the now defunct Council on International Economic Policy (CIEP).

(7) Strengthen the mandate of FEMA as the action arm of the new organization with a clearly established role (and the necessary resources) to develop, coordinate and monitor interagency emergency preparedness programs in the above areas. Specifically:

(a) Establish an improved data base and analytical models on the health of critical defense sectors and, in cooperation with the Council of Economic Advisors and OMB, make five year projections on such sectors with a view to identifying future problems while there is still time for remedial actions.

(b) Provide "national security readiness impact" analyses of all trade policy actions, working with the U.S. Trade Representative (USTR) and the line departments and agencies concerned.

(c) Provide the new National Security Resources Board with options for correcting deficiencies, bottlenecks and critical foreign dependencies, and cost-effectiveness estimates, so that the senior policy body can recommend to the President specific action from among the possibilities arrayed in Section V above.

(8) Publish a list of "endangered industries" which are considered vital to U.S. national security interests along with strategies for public and private sector cooperation to maintain vital production capabilities for emergency purposes under the terms of the Defense Production Act of 1950 and other relevant legislation.

(9) Establish a network of "blue ribbon" panels of industrial expertise for the purpose of providing surveillance of competitive conditions, changes in industrial structure, technological developments and for institutionalizing expertise on emergency preparedness planning. Senior level executives, CEOs and senior vice-presidents of major corporations, would receive presidential appointments to serve in the national interest. During peacetime these groups would provide early warning of problems and would review selective emergency preparedness plans. Under emergency conditions they would assist in facilitating defense production and national resource allocation actions.

Even if the comprehensive and long-range actions recommended here are politically (or fiscally) impractical in the next year or so, a minimum essential step would be the gathering of data and formulation of issues and options by a small planning staff for the incoming administration and its transition team.

If the next administration can succeed in reordering the policy formulation and resource allocation mechanism of the executive branch to incorporate a new realism in balancing strategy and resources it could gain a powerful new lever for influencing the evolving East-West balance, confronting our future adversaries more directly with the economic prowess of the U.S. and its allies. Hopefully, this would encourage the Warsaw Pact to move toward a more cooperative and less confrontational stance in improving long term East-West relations and strategic stability.

APPENDIX A
Charts and Tables

CHART 1
U.S. RELIANCE ON FOREIGN SUPPLIES OF MINERALS

MINERAL	PERCENT IMPORTED IN 1986	MAJOR SOURCES (1982-85)	MAJOR USES
Columbium	100	Brazil, Canada, Thailand, Nigeria	Steelmaking and aerospace alloys
Graphite	100	Mexico, China, Brazil, Madagascar	Metallurgical processes
Manganese	100	South Africa, France, Brazil, Gabon	Steelmaking
Mica (sheet)	100	India, Belgium, France, Japan	Electronic and electrical equipment
Strontium	100	Mexico, Spain	Television picture tubes, pyrotechnics
Platinum group	98	South Africa, Britain, Soviet Union	Catalytic converters for autos, electrical and electronic equipment
Bauxite and alumina	97	Australia, Guinea, Jamaica, Suriname	Aluminum production
Cobalt	92	Zaire, Zambia, Canada, Norway	Aerospace alloys
Diamonds (industrial)	92	South Africa, Britain, Ireland, Belgium	Machinery for grinding and cutting
Tantalum	91	Thailand, Brazil, Australia, Malaysia	Electronic components
Fluorspar	88	Mexico, South Africa, China, Italy	Raw material for metallurgical and chemical industries
Chromium	82	South Africa, Zimbabwe, Turkey, Yugoslavia	Stainless steel
Nickel	78	Canada, Australia, Norway, Botswana	Stainless steel and other alloys
Potash	78	Canada, Israel, East Germany, Soviet Union	Fertilizer
Tin	77	Thailand, Brazil, Indonesia, Bolivia	Cans, electrical construction
Zinc	74	Canada, Mexico, Peru, Australia	Construction and transportation materials
Cadmium	69	Canada, Australia, Mexico, West Germany	Plating and coating of metals
Silver	69	Canada, Mexico, Britain, Peru	Photography, electrical and electronic components
Barite	66	China, Morocco, India, Chile	Oil drilling fluids

Source: U.S. Bureau of Mines

89

CHART 2

NATIONAL DEFENSE STOCKPILE
TOTAL GOALS VS. INVENTORY

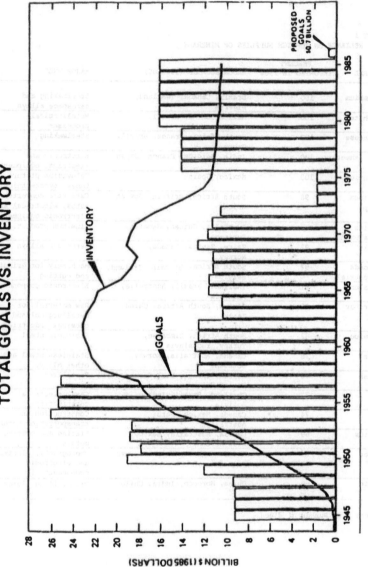

Source: Federal Emergency Management Agency.

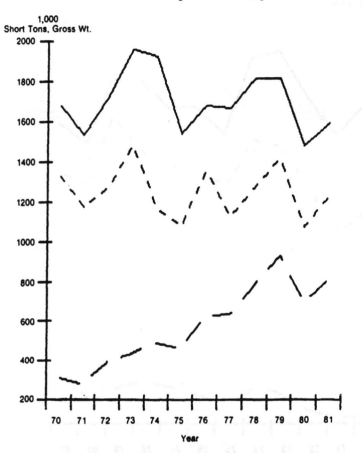

Chart 3—United States Iron and Steel Production Index,
Consumption and Imports of Ferromanganese,
Silicomanganese and Manganese Metal

1,000
Short Tons, Gross Wt.

———— U.S. Industrial Production Index: Iron and Steel
— — — U.S. Apparent Consumption; All Manganese Products
— — Imports: All Manganese Products

Industrial Production Index: 1967 = 1 X 1600 (000) short tons, gross wt.

Source: Compiled from official statistics of Bureau of Mines, data
collected from the Department of Commerce section 232 investigation,
and material provided by Data Resources, Inc., Washington, D.C.

91

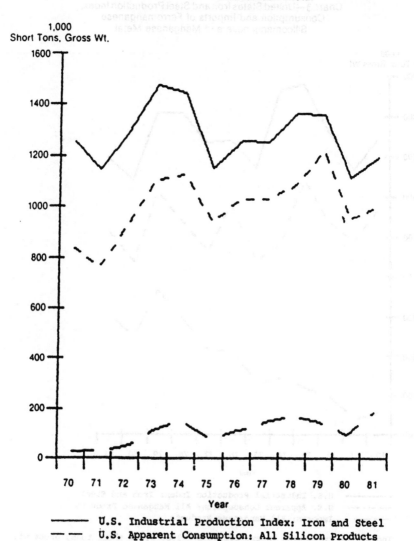

Chart 4—United States Iron and Steel Production Index.
Consumption and Imports of Silicon Ferroalloys
and Silicon Metal

1,000
Short Tons, Gross Wt.

—————— U.S. Industrial Production Index: Iron and Steel
— — U.S. Apparent Consumption: All Silicon Products
— — Imports: All Silicon Products

Industrial Production Index: 1967 = 1 X 1200 (000) short tons, gross wt.

Source: Compiled from official statistics of Bureau of Mines, data collected from the Department of Commerce section 232 investigation, and material provided by Data Resources, Inc., Washington, D.C.

92

CHART 5
STEEL PRODUCT REQUIREMENTS DURING MOBILIZATION AND WAR*

```
DEFENSE REQUIREMENT**                              47
ESSENTIAL CIVILIAN NEEDS***                        94
                                                  ---
                    TOTAL                          141

CURRENT CAPACITY                                   108
SHORTFALL (TO BE MADE UP BY IMPORTS)               33
```

*   Million short tons.

** Defense demand as a proportion of total from DOD
    economic models and an average factor for mobilization
    demand as explained in the section on ferroalloys.

*** Based on the relationship between military demand and
    essential support as estimated in a 1979 FEMA study.

SOURCE: Logistics Management Institute

CHART 6
FERROALLOY DATA

Trends	Ferroalloys SIC (3312, 3339) ($82mil)						
	1980	1981	1982	1983	1984	1985	% Chng
FINANCIAL							
Sales	863.9	833.7	566.0	598.8	703.2	599.2	-44.2%
Shipments T(st)	1200	1146	675	668	795	648	-85.2%
ROA							
PROFIT	-9	12	-105	-65	1	-15	TOTL: -181
D/E							
STRUCTURAL							
Prod. Capacity	1548	1559	1100	1102	1224	1043	-48.4%
Util. Rate *	68.0%	64.0%	37.0%	35.0%	46.0%	39.0%	
Employment (TH)	7.2	6.7	4.9	3.9	4.8	4.1	
DOD Share (Shp)							

COMPETITIVE

Dom. Mkt Share (%Cons)							
S. AFR	23.7%	28.4%	26.0%	21.7%	27.5%		
FRANCE	10.6%	10.2%	9.1%	9.0%	8.6%		
BRAZIL	2.1%	5.7%	7.6%	7.4%	6.9%		
World Mkt Share (%Prod)							
U.S.	8.7%	9.2%	5.4%	5.0%	6.6%		
Jap.	11.7%	11.0%	11.3%	9.2%	9.5%		
USSR	18.7%	20.0%	22.6%	23.7%	22.1%		
S. AFR	10.1%	9.4%	7.9%	9.1%	9.8%		
Productivity $82T(Shp/Emp)							
Cap Exp($82M)	32.7	28.4	20.8	10.6	11.7	19.0	-72.5%
CE/Sales	3.8%	3.4%	3.7%	1.8%	1.7%	3.2%	
Import(%Cons)	47.0%	56.0%	54.0%	59.0%	59.0%	62.0%	

Shipments do not include stockpile conversion
* % KWHR/Capacity
SOURCE: Ferroalloy Association, Washington, D.C.

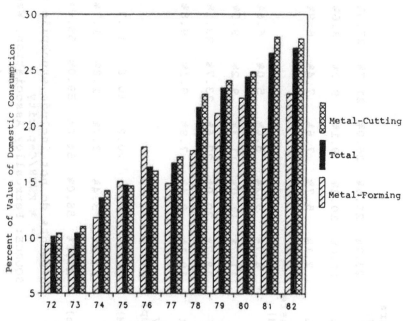

CHART 7
Import Share of Value
of U.S. Domestic Consumption
of Machine Tools
1972-82

1982 data are for first three quarters.

Source: U.S. Department of Commerce, Series IM-146 and EM-522
(monthly), and "Current Industrial Reports" Series MQ-35W,
Metalworking Machinery (quarterly and annual summaries); NMTBA.

96

CHART 8
U.S. Demand (a) for Machine Tools
and Potential Supply (b) of Machine Tools
Under the "Large Conventional War" Scenario
(1972 Dollars), 1988-91

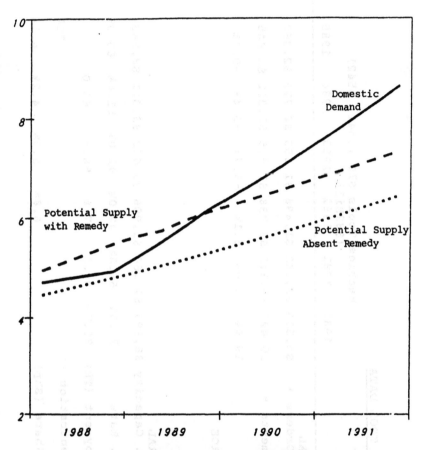

(a) U.S. demand is defined as domestic demand with no exports.
(b) Potential supply with and without Section 232 remedy is
defined as the maximum output of the domestic machine tool
industry under emergency operating conditions, with no imports.

Source: Data Resources, Inc. (1983); NMTBA.

CHART 9
MACHINE TOOL DATA

Machine Tools SIC (3541, 3542)
($82Mil)

Trends	1980	1981	1982	1983	1984	1985	% Chng
FINANCIAL							
New Orders *	$5,515	$3,142	$1,498	$1,653	$2,772	$2,363	-57.0%
Shipments *	$5,422	$5,343	$3,738	$1,936	$2,222	$2,845	-47.5%
ROA	19.4%	18.0%	6.1%	-8.7%	-3.4%	-0.7%	
ROI/ROE							
D/E							
STRUCTURAL							
Prod. Capacity	$6,994	$7,160	$5,906	$3,059	$3,311	$3,983	-43.0%
Util. Rate	71.0%	66.0%	42.0%	42.0%	51.0%	60.0%	
Employment (TH)	99.7	98.3	77.8	58.3	63.0		
Concentration **						75%	
DOD Share (Shp)			6.8%	6.5%	4.2%	4.1%	

COMPETITIVE

Dom. Mkt Share (%Cons)							
Jpn.	9.2%	12.3%	11.9%	15.3%	20.3%	21.3%	
FDR.	4.4%	3.4%	4.6%	4.6%	6.1%	6.2%	
Taiw.	1.7%	1.8%	2.0%	3.1%	2.9%	3.3%	
World Mkt Share (%Prod)							
U.S.	18.1%	19.5%	17.2%	11.2%	12.6%	12.5%	
Jap.	14.4%	18.3%	17.2%	18.5%	23.2%	24.4%	
FDR.		15.9%	16.7%	14.6%	14.6%	14.6%	
Productivity $82T(Shp/Emp)	$54.38	$54.35	$48.05	$33.21	$35.27		-35.1%
Cap Exp($82M)	$280.0	$316.0	$190.3	$129.5			-53.8%
R&D/Sales	4.2%	4.3%	5.5%	7.0%	7.0%		
U.S. Exp(%Prod)	15.3%	18.6%	15.1%	16.7%	15.4%	14.7%	

Source: NMTBA, Dept. of Commerce

* Shipments valued over $2,500
** For top 10 firms

CHART 10
Semiconductor World Market Share
(Percent of World Shipments)

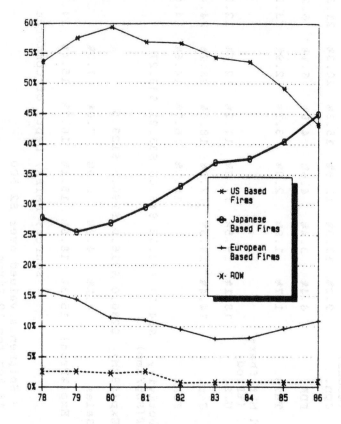

Source: Semiconductor Industry Association.

	U.S. LAG			Parity With Japan	U.S. LEAD		
	Substantial	Clear	Slight		Slight	Clear	Substantial
Silicon Products							
DRAMs		<	•				
SRAMs		<	•				
EPROMs				<	•		
Microprocessors					<•		
Custom, Semicustom Logic					<	•	
Bipolar			<	•			
Nonsilicon Products							
Memory			<		•		
Logic			<			•	
Linear					•<		
Optoelectronics		<	•				
Heterostructures		<	•				
Materials							
Silicon			<	•			
Gallium Arsenide		<		•			
Processing Equipment							
Lithography							
Optical				<	•		
E-Beam				<		•	
X-Ray				<	•		
Ion Implantation Technology					<•		
Chemical Vapor Deposition				•<			
Deposition, Diffusion, Other				<	•		
Energy-Assisted Processing*			<				
Assembly				•<			
Packaging		<•					
Test		<			•		
CAE					<	•	•
CAM		<			•		

* N/A in 1979 - 1980.

• U.S. Position 1979 - 1980 (IQ)
< U.S. Position 1986 - 1987 (IQ)

Source: Semiconductor Industry Association

CHART 12

	Current Status						Outlook

```
                 FINANCIAL                COMP.      NAT SEC.
CASE ST.          STATUS    STRUCTURE    POSITION     ASSMT.
--------1--------1----------1--------1--------1--------------------
Raw Mat. 1   A   1    A     1   P    1   A    1  POOR- High cost
         1       1          1        1        1  domestic production
         1       1          1        1        1
         1       1          1        1        1
Energy   1   A   1    A     1   P    1   A    1  POOR- Growing import
         1       1          1        1        1  dependency
         1       1          1        1        1
         1       1          1        1        1
Fe-Alloys1   P   1    P     1   P    1   P    1  POOR- Rapidly
         1       1          1        1        1  diminishing domestic
         1       1          1        1        1  owned capacity
         1       1          1        1        1
MachTools1   P   1    A     1   P    1   A    1  POOR- Inadequate
         1       1          1        1        1  competitive position
         1       1          1        1        1
         1       1          1        1        1
Semicon  1   G   1    A     1   P    1   G    1  ADEQUATE- Increasing
         1       1          1        1        1  foreign competition
```

G=Good   COMPOSITE STRATEGIC
A=Adequate   INDUSTRY ASSESSMENT
P=Poor

(Based on individual case study matrices)

CHART 13

U.S. Manufactures Trade—Major Product Categories, 1981-1985

	U.S. EXPORTS			U.S. IMPORTS			BALANCE		
	1985 ($bil)	CHANGE fr '84 (%)	CHANGE fr '81 (%)	1985 ($bil)	CHANGE fr '84 (%)	CHANGE fr '81 (%)	1985 ($bil)	CHANGE fr '84 ($ bil)	CHANGE fr '81 ($ bil)
TOTAL TRADE (Imports c.i.f.)	213.1	-2	-9	361.6	6	32	-148.5	-25.2	-108.8
Agricultural Products	29.6	-22	-32	22.0	2	18	7.6	-8.6	-17.1
Manufactured Goods	145.4	2	-6	258.2	11	73	-112.8	-24.0	-118.0
Petroleum Products	4.7	4	27	51.5	-12	-34	-46.8	6.9	28.0
TOTAL TRADE (Imports customs value)	213.1	-2	-9	345.3	6	32	-132.2	-24.3	-104.6
Agricultural Products	29.6	-22	-32	20.0	1	18	9.6	-8.4	-16.7
Manufactured Goods	145.4	2	-6	246.8	11	73	-101.4	-23.0	-113.1
Petroleum Products	4.7	4	27	49.6	-11	-34	-44.9	6.5	27.0
BY "END-USE" DEFINITION (Imports customs value)									
Capital Goods	73.9	3	-8	65.1	9	89	8.8	-3.4	-36.9
Automotive Products	22.9	11	27	66.8	25	125	-43.9	-11.0	-32.2
Consumer Goods	12.6	-5	-20	68.3	14	76	-55.7	-9.0	-32.8
Industrial Supplies & Materials (excluding petroleum)	53.5	-6	-16	63.1	-5	10	-9.6	-0.2	-16.0

MANUFACTURED GOODS BY MAJOR SITC CATEGORIES (Imports customs value)

Chemicals (SITC 5)	21.8	-3	3	14.5	6	54	7.3	-1.4	-4.5
Basic Manufactures (6)—	14.0	-7	-32	46.5	1	25	-32.5	-1.5	-15.8
Paper	2.3	-12	-23	6.0	7	54	-3.7	-0.7	-2.8
Textiles	2.4	0	-33	4.9	9	63	-2.5	-0.4	-3.6
Iron & Steel	1.2	-8	-59	10.3	-6	-8	-9.1	0.5	-0.8
Nonferrous Metals	1.5	-6	-25	7.0	-15	0	-5.5	1.1	-0.5
Machinery & Transport Equipment (7)—	94.3	5	-1	137.3	15	97	-43.0	-13.8	-69.1
Office Machines & Computers	14.9	2	52	11.6	7	222	3.3	-0.5	-2.9
Electrical Machinery & Parts	12.5	-9	9	17.7	-3	92	-5.2	-0.7	-7.5
Power Generating Machinery (including engines)	9.3	2	-2	8.8	21	91	0.5	-1.3	-4.4
Nonconsumer Telecom. Equipment	4.2	8	8	9.5	12	106	-5.3	-0.7	-4.6
Construction & Special Purpose Machinery	8.4	5	-24	6.2	11	63	2.2	-0.2	-5.1
General Industrial Machinery & Parts	7.4	-6	-36	8.1	17	65	-0.7	-1.7	-7.3
Machine Tools & Metalworking Machy.	1.2	0	-45	2.8	40	40	-1.6	-0.8	-1.8
Agricultural Machinery & Tractors	1.6	-6	-54	1.4	-7	8	0.2	0.0	-2.0
Automotive & Transport Equipment—									
Cars	6.0	22	54	36.5	25	109	-30.5	-6.2	-16.9
Automotive Parts	9.4	3	26	10.3	17	151	-0.9	-1.3	-4.4
Aircraft & Parts	14.4	32	2	3.6	20	38	10.8	2.9	-1.3
Miscellaneous Manufactures (8)—	15.3	-3	-8	48.5	14	85	-33.2	-6.4	-23.7
Professional, Scientific & Controlling Instruments	6.5	5	8	3.2	19	88	3.2	-0.2	-1.1
Clothing	0.8	0	-33	14.9	10	99	-14.1	-1.4	-7.4
Toys, Games & Sporting Goods	0.6	-14	-45	4.1	24	86	-3.5	-0.9	-2.4

Source: NAM, from statistics in Commerce Department, *Highlights of U.S. Export and Import Trade.*

CHART 14

Ratio of U.S. Trade to Production and Consumption: Selected Manufactured Goods Categories, 1972-1985

PRODUCT GROUP	EST. TOTAL 1985 U.S. SHIPMENTS	REAL AVG. ANNUAL GROWTH 1972-85	IMPORTS AS SHARE OF DOMESTIC CONSUMPTION			EXPORTS AS SHARE OF DOMESTIC PRODUCTION		
			1972	1981	1985	1972	1981	1985
A. HIGH TECHNOLOGY & ELECTRONIC PRODUCTS								
Computers	$53.4 billion	n.a.%	4%	7%	18%	22%	29%	29%
Semiconductors	14.9	33.7	15	34	40	20	35	32
Instruments								
Engineering & Optical Instruments	9.5	9.2	10	19	16	12	36	26
Measuring & Control Instruments	10.2	5.9	4	5	6	19	21	16
Electricity Measuring Instruments	8.8	9.4	8	12	12	20	31	22
Telephone Equipment	15.4	5.0	2	4	12	7	7	5
Radio-TV Communications Equipment	42.7	7.9	3	7	7	7	9	7
Aerospace—								
Civilian Aircraft	11.4	3.1	2	22	18	28	65	39
Engines	13.5	4.5	6	14	16	19	20	24
Other Aircraft Equipment	14.5	2.3	11	18	19	26	41	39
Photographic Equipment	15.9	3.8	7	15	19	12	16	14
Indust. Inorganic Chemicals	16.1	0.1	10	21	19	18	25	20

B. SELECTED OTHER INDUSTRIES

Electrical Equipment—								
Transformers*	$3.5 billion	-0.3%	3%	6%	10%	3%	8%	6%
Motors & Generators*	7.0	0.1	5	10	16	9	12	10
Machine Tools**	4.2	-3.1	10	27	45	20	20	18
Construction Machinery	12.0	-2.7	2	9	16	28	41	21
Farm Machinery	8.6	-1.8	10	13	20	11	23	22
Oil Field Machinery	6.1	4.6	1	4	1	45	42	52
General Industrial Machinery—								
Internal Combustion Engines	11.8	2.0	6	6	5	15	24	17
Compressors	2.7	3.5	8	9	16	28	32	25
Pumps	5.2	1.4	4	9	10	16	18	17
Motor Vehicles (All types)	97.0	1.0	8	19	20	2	5	2
(Passenger Cars-Units)	—	—	15	27	26	—	—	—
Steel Mill Products***	50.7	-2.6	17	19	24	3	3	1
Household Appliances	15.2	1.2	7	9	15	4	10	6
Household Furniture	16.3	0.6	3	7	14	1	2	1
Radio & TV Sets	7.1	6.1	37	59	63	4	10	8
Footwear—								
Leather Shoes	3.8	-4.3	17	33	58	0	2	3
Rubber & Plastic Shoes#	n.a.	-6.8	28	61	63	—	—	—
Textiles & Apparel—								
Textile Mill Products	54.1	0.9	5	6	7	3	7	3
Man-Made Fibers	9.7	3.7	5	1	3	5	17	11
Apparel	48.0	0.6	7	12	25	1	2	2

*Electrical equipment 1985 data based on unpublished Commerce Department data on industry shipments.
**Machine tool trade ratios based on data in special trade tables and unpublished Commerce Department estimates.
***Steel trade on tonnage basis.
#Domestic industry growth and trade figures based on Commerce Department data for waterproofed and rubber sole/fabric upper shoes.

Source: NAM, from data in Commerce Department, *U.S. Industrial Outlook, 1985* and unpublished data.

CHART 15

Critical Defense Manufacturing Industries

SIC	Description
244	Wood Containers.
281	Industrial Inorganic Chemicals.
286	Industrial Organic Chemicals.
289	Miscellaneous Chemical Products.
329	Abrasive, Asbestos and Miscellaneous nonmetallic mineral products.
331	Blast Furnaces, Steel Works and Rolling and finishing mills.
332	Iron and Steel Foundries.
333	Primary Smelting and Refining of Nonferrous Metals.
334	Secondary Smelting and Refining of Nonferrous metals.
335	Rolling, Drawing and Extruding of Nonferrous metals.
336	Nonferrous foundries (Castings).
339	Miscellaneous Primary Metal Products.
344	Fabricated Structural Metal Products.
345	Screw Machine Products.
346	Metal Forgings and Stampings.
347	Coating, Engraving and Allied Services.
348	Ordnance and Accessories, Except Vehicles and guided missiles.
349	Miscellaneous Fabricated Metal Products.
351	Engines and Turbines.
353	Construction, Mining, and Material Handling machinery and equipment.
354	Metal Working Machinery and Equipment.
356	General Industrial Machinery and Equipment.
357	Office Computing and Accounting Machines.
359	Miscellaneous Machinery Except Electrical.
362	Electrical Industrial Apparatus.
366	Radio and TV Communications Equipment.
367	Electronic Components and Accessories.
371	Motor Vehicles and Motor Vehicle Equipment.
372	Aircraft and Parts.
373	Ship and Boat Building and Repair.
376	Guided Missiles, Space Vehicles and Parts.
379	Miscellaneous Transportation Equipment.
381	Engineering, Laboratory, Scientific and Research instruments and associated equipment.
382	Measuring and Controlling Instruments.
383	Optical Instruments and Lenses.

SOURCE: DEPARTMENT OF COMMERCE

CHART 16

INDUSTRY PERFORMANCE MATRIX   (IPM)

5 / 10 Years	Raw Mat.	Energy	Fe-Alloy	MachTool	Semicon
FINANCIAL					
New Orders					
Shipments					
ROA					
ROI/ROE					
D/E					
STRUCTURAL					
Prod. Cap.					
Util. Rate					
Employmt (TH)					
Concentr.					
DOD Share					

CHART 16 (continued)

5 / 10 Years	Raw Mat.	Energy	Fe-Alloy	MachTool	Semicon

COMPETITIVE
Dom. Mkt Shr
(%Cons)
   Jpn.

   FDR.

   Taiw.

World Mkt Shr
(%Prod)
   U.S.

   Jap.

   FDR.

Productivity

Cap Exp

R&D/Sales

U.S. Exp

NATIONAL SEC ASSMT

    G = GOOD   A = ADEQUATE   P = POOR

THE MOBILIZATION PROCESS

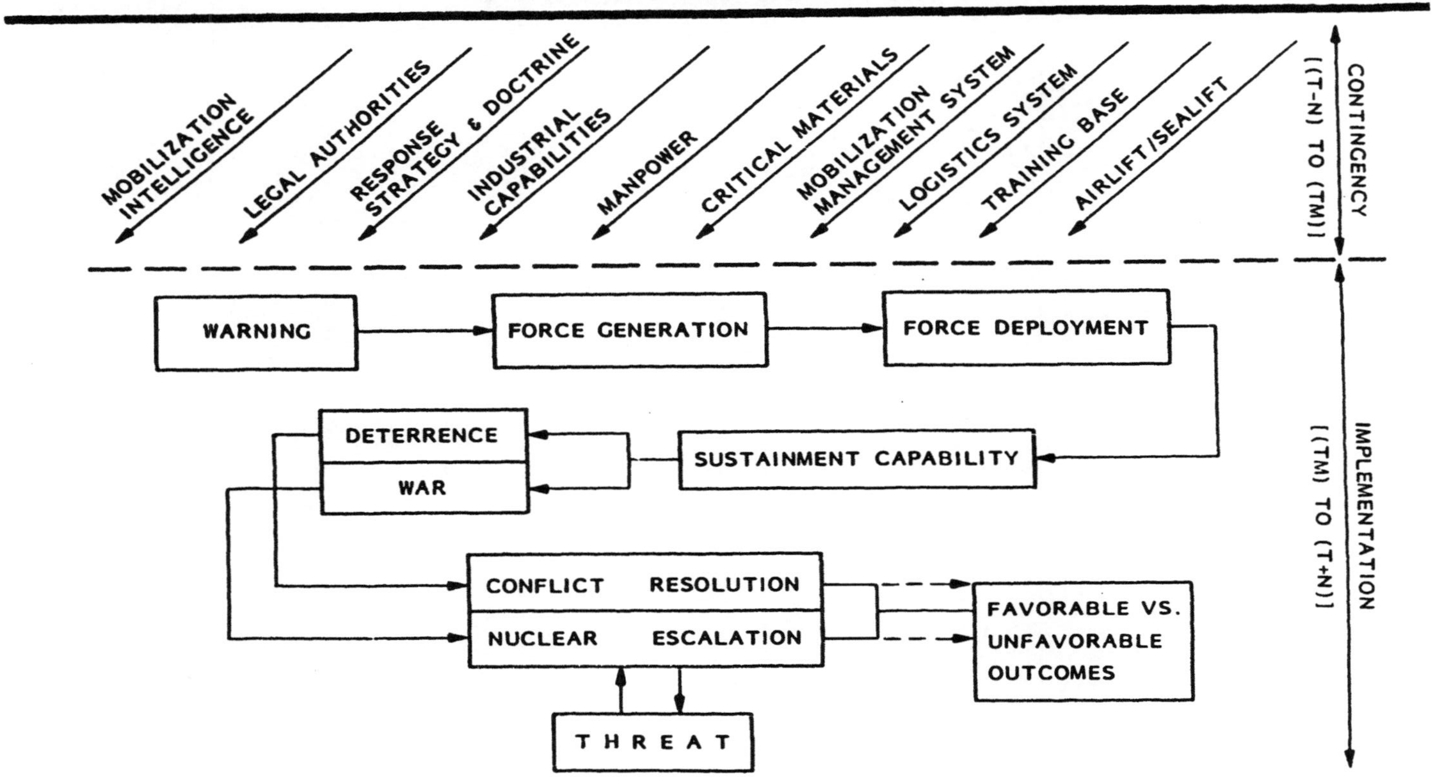

CHART 17

CONTINGENCY
[(T-N) TO (TM)]

IMPLEMENTATION
[(TM) TO (T+N)]

AIRLIFT/SEALIFT
TRAINING BASE
LOGISTICS SYSTEM
MOBILIZATION MANAGEMENT SYSTEM
CRITICAL MATERIALS
MANPOWER
INDUSTRIAL CAPABILITIES
STRATEGY & DOCTRINE
RESPONSE
LEGAL AUTHORITIES
MOBILIZATION INTELLIGENCE

WARNING

FORCE GENERATION

FORCE DEPLOYMENT

SUSTAINMENT CAPABILITY

DETERRENCE

WAR

CONFLICT RESOLUTION

NUCLEAR ESCALATION

THREAT

FAVORABLE VS. UNFAVORABLE OUTCOMES

109

THE MOTIVATION PROCESS

APPENDIX B
Selected Bibliography

Cohen, Steven S. 1987. Manufacturing Matters: The Myth of the Post Industrial Economy, Basic Books, New York, New York.

Danielan, R. L. and S. E. Thomsen. 1987. The Forgotten Deficit: America's Addiction to Foreign Capital, The International Economic Policy Association, Westview Press, Boulder.

The Executive Office of the President. 1987. National Security Strategy of the United States, Washington, D.C.

Federal Emergency Management Agency. Stockpile Report to the Congress, (semi annual), Washington, D.C.

The Fletcher School of Law and Diplomacy. 1981. The U.S. Defense Mobilization Infrastructure: Problems and Priorities- A Conference Report, Cambridge, Massachusetts.

Gansler, Jacques S. 1980. The Defense Industry, The MIT Press, Cambridge, Massachusetts.

Ikle, Fred Charles. 1980. "Preparing for Industrial Mobilization: The First Step Toward Strength", National Security in the 1980's: From Weakness to Strength, edited by W. Scott Thompson, et al., Institute for Contemporary Studies, San Francisco, California.

Jonas, N. 1986. "Special Report: The Hollow Corporation", Business Week, (March 3).

Jones, Norman. 1987. "Can America Compete", Business Week, (April 20).

Karmin, M.W. 1987. "Will the U.S. Stay Number One?" U.S. News and World Report, (February 2).

Manufacturing Studies Board. 1987. Manufacturing Technology Cornerstone of a Renewed Defense Industrial Base, National Academy Press, Washington, D.C.

Manufacturing Studies Board. 1983. The U.S. Machine Tool Industry and the Defense Industrial Base, National Academy Press, Washington, D.C.

Myers, M.G. and D.J. Peterson and R.L. Arnberg. 1986. The Effects of a Loss of Domestic Ferroalloy Capacity, Logistics Management Institute, Bethesda, Maryland.

National Association of Manufacturers. 1986. U.S. Trade Balance at a Turning Point: Can We Eliminate the Trade Deficit by 1990?, Washington, D.C.

National Defense University. 1985. Mobilization Concepts Development Center, H.L. Merritt and L.F. Carter eds., Mobilization and the National Defense, National Defense University Press, Washington, D.C.

National Defense University. 1985. Industrial College of the Armed Forces, Mobilization: What Should be done? What Can Be Done?, Proceedings, Annual Mobilization Conference, May 1985, National Defense University, Washington, D.C.

National Machine Tool Builders Association. 1985. The Economic Handbook of the Machine Tool Industry, Mclean, Virginia.

National Materials Advisory Board. 1985. Basic and Strategic Metals Industries Threats and Opportunities, Report NMAB-425, National Academy Press, Washington D.C.

Olvey, L.D. and H.A. Leonard and B.E. Arlinghaus. 1982. Industrial Capacity and Defense Planning, Lexington Books, Lexington, Massachusetts.

Pfaltzgraff, R.L. and Uri Ra'anan. 1983. The U.S. Defense Mobilization Infrastructure: Problems and Priorities. International Security Studies Program The Fletcher School of Law and Diplomacy, Tufts University, Archon Books, Cambridge Massachusetts.

Stanley, T.W. and R.L. Danielan and S.M. Rosenblatt. 1982. U.S. Foreign Economic Strategy for the Eighties, International Economic Policy Association, Westview Press, Boulder, Colorado.

Stanley, T. W. and John P. Hardt. 1986. Western and Eastern Economic Constraints on Defense, The Atlantic Council and The International Economics Studies Institute, Washington, D.C.

U.S. Department of Commerce. 1987. The U.S. Industrial Outlook: 1987, USDOC-ITA, Washington, D.C.

U.S. Department of Commerce. 1982. Report to the President: The Effect of Imports of Chromium, Manganese and Silicon Ferroalloys and Related Materials on the National Security, USDOC-ITA, Washington, D.C.

U.S. Department of Defense. 1987. Report of the Task Force on Defense Semiconductor Dependency, Defense Science Board, Office of the Secretary of Defense for Acquisition, Department of Defense, Washington, D.C.

U.S. Department of Defense. 1980. Report of the Defense Science Board 1980 Summer Study Panel on Industrial Responsiveness, Office of the Undersecretary of Defense for Research and Engineering, Washington, D.C.

U.S. House of Representatives Committee on Armed Services. 1981. Defense Industrial Base Panel, The Ailing Defense Industrial Base: Unready for Crisis", Committee Print 29, Washington, D.C.

The White House. 1987. The Economic Report of the President, U.S. Government Printing Office, Washington, D.C.

About the Authors

Timothy W. Stanley is president of the International Economic Studies Institute and the former chairman and president of the International Economic Policy Association. He is a lawyer and political economist. His government service, in addition to two military terms of duty, includes the White House Staff, Office of the Secretary of Defense (Policy Planning), Defense Advisor and Minister at the U.S. Mission to the North Atlantic Treaty Organization and Special Representative of the Arms Control and Disarmament Agency at the Vienna negotiations.

He has conducted more than a dozen surveys of Europe and Latin America, written numerous reports, articles and books, testified before various congressional committees, and frequently addressed international forums on international economic issues. Major books which he has written or coauthored include Western and Eastern Economic Constraints on Defense, U.S. Economic Strategy for the Eighties, Raw Materials and Foreign Policy, Technology and Economic Development, The U.S. Balance of Payments, American Defense and National Security, NATO in Transition, and Detente Diplomacy.

He is a member of the State Department Advisory Committee on International Investment and of the National Strategic Materials and Minerals Advisory Committee. He is a director of the Atlantic Council of the U.S., and affiliated with the Council on Foreign Relations, the International Institute for Strategic Studies, the Washington Institute of Foreign Affairs, the Global Economic Action Institute, and the Atlantic Institute Foundation. He has traveled to Russia twice and participates in the Atlantic Council's ongoing dialogue on disarmament with leading Russian officials and scholars.

Dr. Stanley was educated at Yale (B.A.) and Harvard (LL.B. and Ph.D.). He has taught at Harvard, George Washington and Johns Hopkins Universities.

John N. Ellison is senior consultant on national security to the International Economic Studies Institute. He is director of Ellison Associates, a Washington-based consulting firm specializing in strategic planning, national security policy, international economics and space policy for business and government clients engaged in high technology enterprises. He is a member of the Science and Engineering Board of the Coalition for the Strategic Defense

Initiative and a consultant to the National Advisory Commission on Strategic and Critical Materials and Minerals.

For two decades Dr. Ellison served as a strategic economist in the Department of Defense. During the period 1967-78 he was a faculty member and head of economics programs at the Industrial College of the Armed Forces. Following the establishment of the National Defense University in 1977, Dr. Ellison became Associate Dean for Academic Development and a major figure in planning and development of the University. In 1982 he was named Deputy Director and later Director of the Mobilization Concepts Development Center, serving in that position until his retirement from the Department of Defense in 1986. He has also served in the Department of Commerce Office of Strategic Resources.

He is a frequent lecturer at military institutions and civilian colleges and universities in the United States and abroad. He is also a visiting professor at Georgetown and George Washington Universities and the Claremont Graduate School.

Dr. Ellison is a member of numerous professional organizations and a Fellow of the Hudson Institute. He received his B.S. and M.S. degrees in Business Administration from Virginia Polytechnic Institute and the D.B.A. degree in Business Economics from the George Washington University.

His research and publications include works in the field of resource management economics, industrial development, international business, futuristics, economic intelligence and business, and international education programs in relation to national security. He is presently engaged in providing aero-space companies with expertise on economic and technological trends affecting corporate development and international markets.

Jeffrey W. Frumkin is the Senior Research Associate at the International Economic Studies Institute. He received the B.S. degree in Industrial Management and the B.S. degree in Economics from Carnegie-Mellon University. He served an internship with the International Economic Policy Association and the Institute under the The American University's Semester in Washington Program. He has also been an intern in the office of Congressman Gus Yatron.

About the Institute

The Institute was established in 1974, as an independent, non-profit research organization to examine major international economic and related security issues of concern to Americans from a non-partisan, long range, and interdisciplinary perspective.

This particular project is part of a special two-year program being conducted jointly by the Institute and the International Economic Policy Association. IEPA celebrated its 30th anniversary in 1987 as a non-profit tax exempt organization which offers its members analyses of U.S. and foreign government policies affecting international trade, investments, finance, aid and taxation and related political economic developments. The purpose of the special program on "American Business and the World Economy" is to dispel some of the myths that have grown up about the role of business and to identify the challenges and opportunities which lie ahead. The research program highlights the responsibilities of industry both for improving American international competitiveness and for serving as an important element of national security.

In addition to this IESI study and its predecessor, "Western and Eastern Economic Constraints on Defense", the Association has published Jack N. Behrman's The Rise of the Phoenix: The United States in a Restructured World Economy and Ronald L. Danielian and Steven E. Thomsen's The Forgotten Deficit: America's Addiction to Foreign Capital, both in cooperation with Westview Press. The Institute will publish "The Impact of Hostile Takeovers on U.S. Competitiveness" and the Association will issue papers summarizing research on foreign influences on U.S. policymaking.

Index

structure, 57
Defense Science Board, 46,
   48, 49
Task Force of, 50, 52, 53
Defense Systems Acquisition
   Review (DSARC), 72
Department of Defense (DoD),
   xi, 6, 7, 13
   budget formulation and
   resource management of,
   72
   contingency planning system of, 61
   creation of, 85
   and defense industry's low
   rate of return, 74
   and domestic ferrochromium, 33
   and essential defense
   industries, 65-66
   1519 system of, 58-59
   and foreign takeovers, 78
   as industry monitor, 60
   Manufacturing Technology
   Program of, 44
   and national energy
   policy, 24
   planning, programming,
   and budgeting system of,
   57
   procurement processes of,
   57, 72
   and resource allocations,
   63
   rivalries within, 84
   and semiconductor industry, 53
Dirigism, 82
DoD. See Department of
   Defense
Dollar, 12, 59-60
DPA. See Defense Pro-
   duction Act
DRAMs. See Dynamic random-
   access memories
DSARC. See Defense Systems
   Acquisition Review

Dual use equipment, 79
Dynamic random-access
   memories (DRAMs), 48, 49

EEC. See European Econo-
   mic Community
Eisenhower Administration, 6
Eishiro Saito, 36(n53)
Electronics industry, 73
Emergency Economic Powers
   Act, 76
Emergency Mobilization Pre-
   paredness Board (EMPB),
   3, 7, 84-85
EMPB. See Emergency Mo-
   bilization Preparedness
   Board
Energy, 24-27
Energy Security, 24
Environmentalists, 22, 25
Espionage, industrial, 80
European Economic Commu-
   nity (EEC), 36
Export Control Act, 79

Fairchild Industries, 67,
   78
Fair trade, 82
Federal Emergency Manage-
   ment Agency (FEMA),
   xi, 7, 13, 21, 60, 63,
   65, 72, 84, 86, 87
FEMA. See Federal Emer-
   gency Management Agency
Ferroalloy Association, 32
Ferroalloys, 28-37
   domestic production of, 28
   energy costs of, 31
   and national security, 33
   wartime deficit of, 29
   (n40)
Ferrochromium, 20, 30, 31,
   32, 33, 34. See also
   Chromium
Ferromanganese, 20, 30, 31,
   32, 34. See also
   Manganese

120

tional war, 3, 7
and strategic materials,
16
See also Reagan, Ronald
Research and development
(R&D), 73

Santa Fe International Corporation, 78(n)
SDI. See Strategic De-
fense Initiative
Section 232 national security petition(s), 36,
38, 39-42, 66. See
also Trade Expansion
Act
Sematech, 73(n78)
SEMATECH. See Semicon-
ductor Manufacturing
Technology Institute
Semiconductor industry, 14,
46-54
captive vs. merchant
sectors in, 46, 49
growth of, 50-51
in Japan, 48, 49, 50
and Task Force recommendations, 53
and U.S. vs. Japanese
sales, 49
and war materiel produc-
tion, 47
Semiconductor Manufacturing
Technology Institute
(SEMATECH), 53
Sherman Act, 72
SIC. See Standard Indus-
trial Classification
Silicon, 28, 32, 34. See
also Ferrosilicon
South Africa, 17, 31, 34
Southern Africa, 17, 30
South Korea, 11, 51, 61, 70
Soviet Union, vii, viii, 10,
79, 82
SPR. See Strategic Petro-
leum Reserve

Standard Industrial
Classification (SIC),
66
Star Wars. See Strategic
Defense Initiative
State of the Union
Message, 71
Steel industry, 28, 29, 33
Stillwater complex, 22
Stockpile Goals Study,
18-19, 80
Stockpiles
conversion program of,
35-36
and ferroalloys, 32
and lead times, 63
and sales of surplus
materiel, 21
strategic, 21, 32, 80
Stockpile Transaction
Fund, 21, 35
Strategic Air Command, 64
Strategic and Critical
Materials Stock Piling
Revision Act of 1979,
15
Strategic Defense Initia-
tive (SDI), 9
Strategic industries. See
Industries, strategic
Strategic Petroleum Reserve
(SPR), 24, 24(n), 26,
80
Subsidies, 75
Superalloys, 28
Superconductors, 22,
73(n78)
Supply networks, 59
Supply-side theory, 11
Switzerland, 43
Synfuels Corporation, 26

Taiwan, 11, 43, 51, 70
Takeovers, 4(n), 12, 67,
77, 78
Tantalum, 17
Tariffs, 40, 51, 76

Tax incentives, 73-74
Technology transfer, 79-80
Third World, 30, 31, 33, 34
Titanium, 17
Toshiba-IBM incident, 80
Trade Agreements Act of
    1954, 40
Trade Expansion Act, 32, 38,
    66, 76
Trade restrictions, 76-77
Transition Task Force on
    Strategic Materials, 16
Truman, Harry, 6

United States
    balance of payments defi-
        cits of, 11, 78
    capital investment in pro-
        duction technology in,
        52
    conventional capabilities
        of, 8, 58, 60, 61, 82,
        83
    counter-intelligence
        activities of, 80
    as debtor nation, 11-12
    Department of Commerce,
        13, 16, 32, 38, 60, 66,
        72
    Department of Defense.
        See Department of
        Defense
    Department of Interior,
        72, 78(n)
    dependency on foreign
        suppliers, 23, 32, 38,
        53, 56, 61-62
    economic competitiveness
        of, 11, 12-13, 52, 56,
        59
    and energy costs in sili-
        con production, 34
    ethical values of, 13
    ferroalloy imports of,
        31, 34
    ferroalloy industry
        trends in, 36

    fiscal deficits of, 2,
        11, 26, 78, 84
    foreign-based firms of,
        61-62(n)
    and foreign ore depo-
        sits, 29-30, 35
    and high technology
        industries, 59
    House Armed Services
        Committee, 58
    industrial base of, viii
    vs. Japanese interest
        rates, 50
    vs. Japan for semi-
        conductor market, 49
    as leader in research
        and development, 56
    market share losses of,
        59
    mass production in, 52
    mineral imports of, 17
    and national economic
        policy goals, 71-72
    national industrial
        policy debate in, 69
    natural resources of, 22
    National Security Coun-
        cil. See National
        Security Council
    national security vs.
        international economic
        interests, 82
    national security vs.
        resource availability,
        1, 9, 43
    oil imports of, 25, 35
    presidential emergency
        powers of, 63
    reserve forces of, 60, 62
    revenues of, 84
    and service-oriented
        economies, 82
    skilled labor base in, 55
    Supreme Court, 12
    technical education in,
        52, 55
    technological malaise of,

For Product Safety Concerns and Information please contact our
EU representative GPSR@taylorandfrancis.com Taylor & Francis
Verlag GmbH, Kaufingerstraße 24, 80331 München, Germany